How to Value Players
for
Rotisserie®
Baseball
Second Edition

ART McGEE

Edited by
Andy Andres and Skip Snow

Shandler Enterprises, LLC
Roanoke, VA

Shandler Enterprises, LLC
P.O. Box 20303
Roanoke, VA 24018

Offices   540-772-6315
Fax   540-772-1969
Customer service 800-422-7820

E-mail   info@baseballhq.com
Internet   http://www.baseballhq.com/books/htv.shtml

Cover design by Jon Resh@Go-Undaunted.com

ISBN 1-891566-90-3
Printed in the United States of America

Acknowledgments

Many people helped to shepherd this book through the process from First Edition concept to Second Edition finished product. I would especially like to thank Larry Borowsky, editor of the first edition, for his excellent contribution in making the book a clearer and more interesting read. Many thanks also to Scott Morris for his valuable feedback, especially on technical matters. I am grateful to Andy Andres, Skip Snow, and particularly Ron Shandler for their editorial and publishing support in producing this second edition. And thanks to all of the members of the Chicago HardCore League, who have been worthy and fun rivals for almost two decades. Most of all, I would like to thank Elaine, medical consultant to the Art Institutes, for her unflagging support.

CONTENTS

INTRODUCTION
The Objectives of this Book

It's midway through your Rotisserie league's 2006 auction. You have holes to fill everywhere — five on the pitching staff, four on offense — and a dwindling supply of cash. A rival owner nominates catcher Brian McCann. McCann is coming off his MLB debut the previous season — 5 HRs and a .278 batting average in 180 AB in part-time duty after being called up from AA — and he seems to have the everyday job locked up for 2006. On the other hand, he is only 22 years old and has never played in AAA. The bidding creeps up to $8 and the room falls silent. You need a catcher, but there are many better hitters still available, as well as some starting pitchers and closers. Are you better off saving your money to bid on those players? Or should you go ahead and bid $9 for McCann?

You look at the spreadsheet you have prepared for the auction. It includes a forecast of McCann's likely stats for the upcoming season (factoring in higher risk because of his age and lack of experience). More importantly, the spreadsheet tells you the exact number of points those stats are expected to be worth in the final standings. It also accounts for the value of having a productive hitter like McCann at catcher, a notoriously talent-scarce position, and for the value you might reap from having McCann on your roster at a low salary next year. All those types of value have been gathered together and converted into a single dollar value. That value, your spreadsheet says, is $13. At $9, McCann is an excellent bargain. You bid $9, and the other owners let you have him at that price.

McCann goes on to bat .333 with 24 HRs and 93 RBI, and he's one of the main reasons you win your league. Better yet, with him on your roster for two more years at $9, you're looking even stronger for 2007 and 2008.

* * *

This book is about how to value players for Rotisserie baseball — how to quantify all the types of value a player brings to your team and weigh them against each other. The ability to make fine distinctions among players who seem, on the surface, to be worth roughly the same amount is part intuition and part number-crunching. Intuition is mainly a matter of experience, but number-crunching you can learn. This book will teach you how to crunch numbers and how to use that analysis to beat your rival Rotisserie owners.

The key to winning your league is to acquire as much talent as possible in your league's auction. Your success at this task depends on two skills: player forecasting and performance valuation. In other words, you have to have accurate forecasts of how players will perform in the coming season, and you have to know what you should pay for those expected performances in the auction. By purchasing players who are available for less than their fair dollar value, you can stock your roster with the most talent possible. The owner who knows how to get the most value for his dollars has the best chance of finishing in first place come October.

The vast majority of Rotisserie analysts focus almost exclusively on the first of these two skills – player forecasting. They try to answer questions like: Who will get at bats at third base for the Indians this year? Can Joey Gathright hit well enough to stick in the majors? Is Kevin Millwood capable of winning 15 games again?

Roto owners find themselves awash in information for player forecasting. Annual books and magazines review past performances and attempt to project future trends. Television sports stations broadcast virtually every game and sports news shows analyze every baseball development. Internet-based services report and dissect every notable game performance, every transaction and every injury. These information resources are a boon to baseball fans and Roto owners, but, because of their ready availability, they are unlikely to give you an edge in your league. On the contrary, you will need this player forecasting information just to stay even with your rivals. Owners can find a competitive advantage, though, by turning to the second key skill — valuation — that is, the process of calculating accurate dollar values for a given level of performance and potential.

Valuation has become critical to individual Roto owners for another reason. Most published dollar values for players are based on a standard Roto format. However, many, if not most, leagues do not conform to these "official" rules of Roto. Some leagues have fewer than 12 teams. Some deviate from the eight standard scoring categories. Some mix American and National League players. And so on. Each league has its own quirks that affect player values, and published values simply can't reflect these. Yet if your league has only 10 teams, values designed for a 12-team league will be quite misleading. An owner who understands valuation methods can determine appropriate values for his or her league, regardless of its particular rules. If you know how to make the proper adjustments for a 10-team league, for example, then you will have a significant edge over rivals who rely on published values.

Finally, published dollar values, especially those in books and magazines, are often out of date by the time you and the other owners in your league are reading them; injuries, trades and spring training performances have changed the picture considerably. If you have an accurate way of updating and adjusting your dollar values right up until the day of the auction, you will have another edge over your opponents.

For all of these reasons, Roto owners who do a better job in performance valuation will have a decisive advantage over their competitors. The opportunity to gain an advantage in player valuation exists because very little attention has been paid to this area since the early days of Rotisserie. After the initial methods for player valuation were published in the late 1980s, it was as if almost everybody decided, "OK, this is good enough."

As someone who has spent over two decades trading financial instruments for a living, I have an endless fascination with trying to figure out just how much — exactly — things should be worth. After years of tinkering with my methods, I've been able to discover solutions to the problems of Roto performance valuation that I don't think anyone else has found. They've worked in my own Roto leagues, and they can work for you too.

The purpose of this book, then, is to describe my performance valuation methods in sufficient detail so that you can understand them and apply them yourself. I'm not going to tell you what I think each player is worth; my values would be outdated by the time you read them anyway. Instead, I'm going to try to give you the ability to take your own or somebody else's player performance forecasts and convert them into the most accurate dollar values possible. I'll even describe how to set up a spreadsheet to do it. Even if you're not the spreadsheet type, this book will still improve your ability to recognize and quantify value and make your Rotisserie team a perennial contender.

* * *

Now, a few words about how this book is organized. In Part I, I present my basic method for performance valuation: Marginal SGP Pricing. I play in a league based on the "official" rules originally published in Rotisserie League Baseball, edited by Glen Waggoner (the book that started the Roto craze in the 1980s), and my methods are tailored to those rules. If your league uses somewhat different rules, the basic method will still apply, as long as you have an auction with a fixed budget to fill your rosters at the start of the season.

Marginal SGP Pricing starts with the "official" rules, then breaks with them by making two major assumptions:

Assumption #1: Other than trades, there are no player transactions during the season. No players can be added to active rosters from reserve rosters or the free agent pool.

Assumption #2: No player carryover to next year. Next season, you start with a clean slate.

Of course, practically nobody plays in leagues with these two restrictions, and in Part II of the book they are dropped. But I start off with these two assumptions to simplify the problem of valuing players. Even in the basic version of Marginal SGP Pricing, I think you'll find intriguing answers to long-time Roto riddles, such as whether you should pay more for a good hitter or a good starting pitcher, or how you can produce precise values to reflect position scarcity (that is, if a catcher and an outfielder have the same expected stats, how much more is the catcher worth?).

In Part II, we remove these two assumptions. We consider what happens when teams can remove and add players to their roster during the season and carry them over for one or more seasons. In the world of finance, opportunities like these are called options, and options have value, sometimes a lot of value. Researchers in the financial markets have devoted enormous effort to understanding and valuing options, and we can apply some of that theory to performance valuation in Roto. In Part II, I'll talk about how to apply options theory and explain Option-Adjusted Marginal SGP Pricing.

In the course of describing my pricing methods, I borrow a number of terms from the world of finance and economics, and I make up many new terms of my own. In order to give you a quick reference for all of the terminology, I have included a glossary at the end of the book.

* * *

Before we forge ahead, we should quickly review the characteristics of a Rotisserie league. For purposes of illustration, we will use a Roto league that employs only American League players. A standard AL-only league comprises 12 teams, and each team has 23 players on its active roster. Therefore, a total of 276 roster slots (12 * 23) must be filled on auction day.

Each team's 23 players must consist of 14 hitters and nine pitchers. Furthermore, the 14 hitters must include two catchers, one first baseman, one second baseman, one shortstop, one third baseman, five outfielders, one corner infielder (who can play either first base or third base), one middle infielder (who can play either second base or shortstop), and one designated hitter or utility player (who can play any position other than pitcher). Since all 12 teams must meet these requirements, the following numbers of slots at each position must be filled in the auction:

24 catchers,
12 first basemen,
12 second basemen,
12 shortstops,
12 third basemen,
60 outfielders,
12 corner infielders,
12 middle infielders, and
<u>12 designated hitters or utility players</u>

equals 168 hitters
plus <u>108 pitchers</u>
equals 276 total players.

Each team has $260 to spend, so the total amount that all 12 teams can spend in the auction is $3120 (12 * $260).

If you're playing with reserve rosters, then after each team has acquired its 23-man active roster in the auction, the reserve draft begins. The reserve draft is a simple rotation draft, with team owners selecting players in turn for a predetermined number of rounds. Owners pay nothing to acquire their reserve players, but these players may be assigned a salary for future seasons, depending upon the round of their selection.

During the season and at the end of the season, league standings are determined by ranking the 12 teams in each of eight statistical categories. Hitters contribute to four categories — home runs, runs batted in, stolen bases, and batting average — and pitchers contribute to four — wins, saves, earned run average, and WHIP (walks plus hits allowed divided by innings pitched). The team that ranks highest in a category earns 12 points in that category, the team that ranks second earns 11 points, and so on. A team's total points across all eight categories determine its place in the overall standings.

Throughout this book, I will refer to the characteristics of this standard 12-team league. For example, I might refer to the worst pitcher purchased in the auction draft as the 108th-best pitcher, or I might refer to the $3120 available to be spent in the draft. If your league has different characteristics (a different number of teams, a different spending limit, etc.), just substitute the appropriate value for your league.

PART ONE
Marginal SGP Pricing

CHAPTER 1
Expected Stats

This book is about how to take forecasts of player stats and convert them into dollar values for your Roto auction. It is not about how to forecast player performance. It assumes that the stats being forecast for each player represent the average anticipated performance for that player in each category in the coming season.

In other words, when you forecast a particular stat for a particular player — say, wins for Johan Santana — you need to think about all of the possible scenarios that may unfold for Santana in the coming season and average them together. Maybe Santana will win 25 games and another Cy Young Award. Maybe (I sure hope not) Santana will have pain in his arm on Opening Day, miss the rest of the season, and not earn a single win. You have to weigh all of these possibilities and make a judgment as to how many games Santana is likely to win on average. You may decide 18 wins is the appropriate average value. I might say 16. Someone else might say 20. Not everyone will have the same opinion. The important thing is to account for all possibilities, good and bad, in making your judgment.

I use the term "expected stats" to describe the required performance forecasts because the word "expected" has a very specific meaning in finance. You may be familiar with the phrase "expected value." Expected value is synonymous with the "weighted mean" or "weighted average" of an uncertain event. You can calculate expected value by attaching a probability (expressed as a fraction of one) to each possible outcome, then adding up the product of each outcome times its probability. Consider the simple case of a coin toss in which you will win $1 if the outcome is heads and $5 if the outcome is tails. (Wouldn't that be nice?) The probability the coin will come up heads is 0.5, and the probability of tails is also 0.5. The expected value of that coin toss for you is (0.5 * $1) + (0.5 * $5) = $0.50 + $2.50 = $3.

For more complex calculations of expected value, the formula is:

Expected value = (probability1 * outcome1) +
(prob2 * outcome2) + . . . + (probN * outcomeN),

where 1 through N represent each of the possible outcomes. Remember, probabilities 1 through N must add up to 1.0.

You could perform the same type of calculation for Johan Santana's wins. If I were doing it, I would attach low probabilities to each possible number of wins from zero to about 10. In the low teens, the probabilities would start increasing. The highest probabilities would be in the mid-teens to about 20. Then the probabilities would start declining again in the low twenties. The probability would fall to zero around 30 wins.

I'm not suggesting that you actually complete this tedious process for each stat for each player available in the auction; if you did, you might have time to develop stat forecasts for, oh, 10 or 12 players before the auction. The point is not that you should mathematically derive an expected value for each player; the point is to think in terms of expected values when you come up with stat forecasts for each player. You should not be thinking, "This forecast is how many wins Santana will get if everything goes well" nor "This is how many wins Scott Baker will get if he cracks the Twins' rotation this year." You should be thinking, "All things considered, on average, this player can be expected to win this many games (or hit this many homers or steal this many bases) this year."

I know that some Roto owners prefer to think about what a player might do in a more positive scenario, especially in the case of marginal players. For example, all other things being equal, they believe a starting pitcher who has, say, a 50 percent chance of getting 10 wins but a 50 percent chance of getting zero wins (depending on whether he makes the rotation or gets sent down to the minors) is worth more than a journeyman middle reliever who gets 5 wins year in, year out. These owners reason that they should give more weight to the 10-win scenario for the first pitcher. I agree that the first pitcher is worth more, for reasons that I discuss in Part II; in forecasting stats, however, I would forecast both pitchers for 5 wins.

The purpose of Marginal SGP Pricing is to calculate the dollar value each player will produce on average in the coming season. If you don't consistently use averages for your stat forecasts, then this method will produce inconsistent values. So for the rest of this book, when I talk about using stat forecasts to calculate dollar values, think "expected stats."

Before we continue, let me reemphasize the importance of stat forecasting. My valuation method gives you the best dollar values based on your expected stats, but it cannot make up for poor stat forecasts. Admittedly, generating expected stats for the hundreds of players eligible for your auction can be a tiresome task. If you want to avoid producing all of these forecasts yourself, you can find plenty of publications and Web sites that will provide forecasts for you. Some forecasters even make their stats available in a form that you can load directly into your spreadsheet, so you do not have to type them in. If you use someone else's forecasts, though, review them to make sure that the forecaster is providing something like expected stats, not best-case scenarios or some other estimate.

CHAPTER 2
Standings Gain Points

The first and most fundamental challenge in converting a player's expected stats into his auction dollar value is to find some way to equate the value of performance in the different Rotisserie categories. Are 20 home runs worth more or less than 90 RBI? How much more or less? What about 20 home runs versus 10 wins? How can we compare stats in counting categories, like home runs or wins, to stats in rate categories, like batting average or ERA?

These are complicated and challenging questions. In the late 1980s, Alex Patton came up with a straightforward and elegant answer (at least, he was the first to publish this answer, as far as I know). To paraphrase, Patton said: Roto standings are determined by the points scored in each category, and a point in one category is just as good as a point in any other. Therefore, if we can accurately estimate, for each category, the production that is likely to gain a team one extra point, we can convert stats in all categories to a common unit. He calls these common units "standings gain points"; I call them SGPs, for short. (Many of the concepts I cover in this and the next chapter were originally presented in Patton's annual books on Roto pricing.)

The Rotisserie scoring categories are of two basic types. Five of the eight categories (HRs, RBI, SBs, wins, and saves) are calculated simply by counting up the number of times a player accomplishes the feat. I will refer to these as the "counting stats" or "counting categories." The other three categories (BA, ERA, and WHIP) are based on rates of performance. They measure the frequency with which a stat occurs per number of opportunities: hits per at-bat, earned runs per nine innings pitched, and walks plus hits per inning pitched. I will call these the "rate stats" or "rate categories."

The counting stats are easier to work with. Let's take the RBI category as an example. We may estimate that it will take about 28 extra RBI to gain one additional standings point in that category at season's end. That is, if we could change nothing else about our team but somehow add 28 RBI, we would expect to finish with one more point in the overall standings. Twenty-eight RBI would equal one SGP. In the home run category, however, it may take only 8 more dingers to move up a notch. In that case, 8 HRs would also be worth one SGP, and the 8 HRs would be equivalent in value to 28 RBI. The values in this chapter are used only as examples. In the next chapter, we'll discuss how to come up with the most accurate estimates for these values for your league.

We can call these values — 8 HRs, 28 RBI — "SGP denominators." When we convert expected stats to SGPs in the counting categories, we simply divide the expected stat by these values. Suppose we expect Miguel Tejada to hit 24 home runs. To convert that into SGPs, we just divide by our SGP denominator:

24 (expected HRs) / 8 (SGP denominator) = 3.0 SGPs

In short, we expect Miguel Tejada's home runs to be worth 3 points in the final standings.

As with expected stats, it's important to think in terms of "average" when selecting SGP denominators. Obviously, the actual benefit a team will gain from Tejada's 24 HRs will vary greatly from team to team and league to league. For a team already leading the HR category, the 24 HRs have no value in the standings. For a team close behind several other teams in that category, 24 more HRs may be worth 5 or 6 points. But going into the auction, when all 12 teams are starting with a blank slate, using an average is the only appropriate way to value players.

Converting expected stats to SGPs is straightforward for the five counting categories — we just divide the expected stat by the SGP denominator. But what about the three rate categories? The concept is the same, but the calculation is more complicated. We still need to estimate how much more batting average it will take to move up one notch in that category. Perhaps it's .002, or two batting average points. But how do we figure out just what kind of individual performance amounts to two more batting average points? The answer depends on four variables: how many at-bats and hits the team already has before we consider the individual player in question, and the expected at-bats and hits for that player. If we have all four of those values, then we can add up the hits, divide by the total at-bats, and compare the resulting average to what the team had without that player.

Table 2-1 shows a simple example. Travis Hafner is expected to add .003 to the team's batting average, raising it from .270 to .273. If (as we assumed above) the SGP denominator for BA is .002, then Hafner's batting average is worth 1.5 SGPs.

Table 2-1

	AB	H	Bat Avg
Team without Travis Hafner	4500	1215	0.270
Travis Hafner	500	150	0.300
Team total	5000	1365	0.273

The concept for batting average is similar to that for HRs, RBI, and SBs, but we need to estimate more numbers. For each position player, we need to come up with two expected stats, not just one. We need to estimate both his expected number of at-bats and his expected number of hits. In addition, we need to estimate two other numbers: the expected number of at-bats and hits of the average team. We'll talk more in the next chapter about how to estimate these last two numbers.

Calculating SGPs for ERA and WHIP requires a similar set of estimates. For each pitcher, in addition to coming up with expected wins and saves, we need to estimate expected innings pitched, earned runs allowed, and walks plus hits allowed. We also need to estimate the expected number of innings pitched, earned runs allowed, and walks plus hits allowed for the average team.

Once we have defined the SGP denominators and the other values that we need for BA, ERA, and WHIP, we can take any player's expected stats and convert them into a single number: SGPs. Then we have a common unit for comparing the production of all hitters and pitchers. In the next chapter, we'll consider how to come up with the best estimates for the denominators and other values needed to make these calculations.

Chapter 2 Postscript: Negative SGPs

Notice one major difference between the counting categories and the rate categories: In the counting categories, players cannot produce negative SGP performances. The worst they can do in categories like HRs and wins is zero. In the rate categories, though, players can produce negative SGPs. In fact, any player who is below the league average in BA, ERA, or WHIP will produce negative SGPs in that category, because that player will hurt the performance of the average team in the category. Furthermore, by definition, the value of players below the league average must exactly offset the value of those players above. Therefore, the total SGPs for all players must be zero in each of these three categories.

When Alex Patton reached the conclusion that the total value in these three categories is zero, he created something of a controversy in Roto circles. Other analysts, like John Benson, disagree with Patton on this point, but I agree with his conclusion. In future chapters, I will discuss other implications of this result.

CHAPTER 3
Estimating SGP Denominators

The best way to estimate how much production it will take to gain a point in each of the statistical categories in your Roto league is to look at the actual results of other leagues. In years past, many Internet-based stat services allowed open access to information on all of their leagues, so this kind of data was easy to acquire. Now, many of these services have restricted access, so you may find it harder to obtain this data yourself.

To start our analysis of SGP denominators, let's take a hypothetical set of AL-only Roto leagues that follow the standard format. For each category, we can calculate the average stat for teams that finished first, teams that finished second, and so on. Computing the average values for the home run category based on these leagues, we find the results displayed in Table 3-1.

Table 3-1

Team Rank in Home Runs	Points in Home Runs	Team Total Home Runs
1	12	225
2	11	214
3	10	204
4	9	190
5	8	183
6	7	178
7	6	172
8	5	160
9	4	157
10	3	145
11	2	135
12	1	114

Next we estimate the average difference between teams in this category. We do so by running a simple regression of home runs on standing points. Regression is a statistical technique for solving this problem, and a regression function is available in most spreadsheet software. To perform the regression calculation above using Microsoft Excel, you can enter the standings points in cells B1 through B12 of a spreadsheet, and then enter the corresponding home run totals in cells C1 through C12. Finally, in another cell in the spreadsheet, enter the formula "=SLOPE(C1:C12,B1:B12)". This formula should produce a value of 9.04. The regression tells us that, based on the average of these hypothetical leagues, a team would require 9.04 additional home runs to gain one additional point in the standings.

It might appear simpler to estimate the average difference between teams by adding up the differences between each pair of adjacent teams (i.e., between first and second place, second and third, etc.) and dividing by 11. This result, however, would be identical to the result you'd get by taking the difference between the first and last-place team and dividing by 11; therefore, it would really only measure two values, those of the first- and last-place teams. Using a regression, which depends on all 12 values, is a superior method.

Does the sample regression mean that you should use 9.04 as the SGP denominator for home runs in your league? Not so fast. We should consider a couple of factors before concluding that these leagues provide a good forecast of what *your* league's standings will look like.

One factor to consider is variations between the American League and the National League. Because of certain differences between the two major leagues, particularly the designated hitter rule, results in AL-based Roto leagues tend to differ from those of NL-based leagues. For all categories, it is essential to recognize any difference between the two major leagues and use data from the appropriate one.

Another important factor is that individual Roto leagues may vary significantly from the averages computed above. For example, although the *average* difference between teams in the above sample was 9.04 HRs — that is, it took about 9 additional home runs to gain a point in the standings — the values for the individual leagues might vary anywhere between 6 and 12. Higher values would indicate HRs were more spread out; lower values would indicate a tighter race.

The variation among these leagues provides some sense of the range of values that we might use if we could calculate SGP denominators at the end of the season. At the start of the season, though, the best we can do is to make an estimate based on a typical value.

SGP Denominators for Rate Categories

The process of determining SGP denominators is essentially the same for each of the other seven categories in standard Roto as for HRs, except that we need to estimate additional values for the three rate categories: batting average, ERA, and WHIP. For each of these three categories, we begin, as before, by running a regression on the results of actual leagues to estimate the average difference between teams at the end of the season. Table 3-2 is analogous to Table 3-1, except that it displays the average values in batting average for the first- through 12th-place teams in our hypothetical set of AL Roto leagues.

Table 3-2

Team Rank in Batting Ave.	Points in Batting Ave.	Team Batting Ave.
1	12	0.2801
2	11	0.2779
3	10	0.2766
4	9	0.2746
5	8	0.2738
6	7	0.2702
7	6	0.2696
8	5	0.2684
9	4	0.2649
10	3	0.2636
11	2	0.2617
12	1	0.2603

The regression on this data produced a value of 0.00182, or just a shade under two batting average points, for the average difference between teams in the standings.

As we discussed in the last chapter, in order to calculate the impact of a player on a team's total in a rate category, we must make an assumption about that team's performance before we add the stats of the player in question. To do so, we must assume that the team has a slot open for that player. Therefore, we estimate the performance of a typical team *before it acquires its last hitter or pitcher* — i.e., a team with 13 hitters or with 8 pitchers. Only then can we calculate how much that last player raises (or lowers) the team in the standings for that category.

Again, we can use sample data to determine appropriate values. Suppose the average AL Rotisserie team compiled 1585 hits in 5869 at-bats, for a .2701 batting average. If we assume that a team has only 13 of its 14 hitting slots filled, we multiply these values by 13/14, or 0.9286, resulting in 1471.8 hits in 5449.8 at-bats. These calculations are summarized in Table 3-3.

Table 3-3

	At-bats	Hits
Average full AL team	5869	1585
Scaled to 13 hitters (* 13/14)	5449.8	1471.8

In other words, when the average team has filled all of its hitting slots except one, it has expected stats of 1471.8 hits in 5449.8 at-bats. To calculate the SGPs that any hitter will add in batting average, we add that hitter's expected hits and at-bats to these totals, then recompute the team's batting average and subtract .2701. Finally, we divide the difference by the SGP denominator for batting average (estimated as 0.00182 in the regression above).

We follow the same procedure to get values for innings pitched, earned runs allowed, and walks plus hits allowed to be used for ERA and WHIP calculations. However, we multiply by 8/9 rather than 13/14 because a team has only nine pitching slots. We arrive at values of 1050 innings pitched, 484.2 earned runs allowed, and 1386 walks plus hits.

For years, I analyzed sample leagues and reviewed a variety of other data to refine annual estimates for SGP denominators, and I published my SGP denominators on the BaseballHQ.com web site before each season. More recently, Gerald Holmes of Baseball HQ has performed this annual update. Following are the SGP denominators published on Baseball HQ for each of the eight "standard" categories in the AL and the NL before the 2006 season:

AMERICAN LEAGUE

HR SGP $=$ HR / 9.5

RBI SGP $=$ RBI / 29.6

SB SGP $=$ SB / 7.6

BA SGP $=$ $(((1472 + \text{Hits}) / (5450 + \text{AB})) - 0.2701) / 0.00182$

Wins SGP $=$ Wins / 3.4

SV SGP $=$ SV / 6.3

ERA SGP $=$ $(4.15 - ((484.2 + \text{ER}) / ((1050 + \text{IP}) / 9))) / 0.067$

WHIP SGP $=$ $(1.32 - ((1386 + \text{H} + \text{BB}) / (1050 + \text{IP}))) / 0.011$

NATIONAL LEAGUE

HR SGP $=$ HR / 9.5

RBI SGP $=$ RBI / 27.3

SB SGP $=$ SB / 7.9

BA SGP $=$ $(((1504 + \text{Hits}) / (5550 + \text{AB})) - 0.271) / 0.0015$

Wins SGP $=$ Wins / 3.1

SV SGP $=$ SV / 6.2

ERA SGP $=$ $(4.06 - ((541.3 + \text{ER}) / ((1200 + \text{IP}) / 9))) / 0.082$

WHIP SGP $=$ $(1.33 - ((1596 + \text{H} + \text{BB}) / (1200 + \text{IP}))) / 0.016$

NL-based Roto leagues draw their rosters from 16 major league teams versus only 14 in the AL, so NL leagues often use 25-man rosters made up of 15 position players and 10 pitchers. The NL formulas above assume the use of these larger rosters. Therefore, compared to the AL equations based on 23-man rosters, the NL BA formula assumes somewhat more team at-bats and the ERA and WHIP formulas assume more team innings pitched.

Many leagues have added categories beyond the standard eight, and three categories in particular have gained broad popularity: runs scored for hitters, and strikeouts and innings pitched for pitchers. Because these three categories are widely used, I can also provide SGP denominators for them:

American League

R SGP =	R / 27.9
K SGP =	K / 39.3
IP SGP =	IP / 40.5

National League

R SGP =	R / 30.2
K SGP =	K / 37.5
IP SGP =	IP / 39.6

Once you have these equations and expected stats set up in a spreadsheet — and we will discuss how to do that in Chapter 7 — you can make adjustments to the denominators as you see fit. If you have been in the same Roto league for a few years with mostly the same group of competitors, you may want to analyze the history of SGP denominators in your own league. For example, if a couple of owners in your league always punt saves, then you may want to increase the denominator in the equation for saves. If you find that your league has tended to have close finishes in home runs, you may want to lower your SGP denominator accordingly.

Applying SGP Denominators to a Sample Player

With SGP denominators in place, we can now make a precise estimate of how many points in the standings a player's expected level of performance is worth. Let's take an example. Before the 2006 season, suppose I assigned the following expected stats to Vladimir Guerrero in the four standard offensive categories:

AB	H	BA	HR	RBI	SB
549	176	.321	34	113	15

As a first step, we calculate Guerrero's expected impact on team batting average, as we did for Travis Hafner in the last chapter. Guerrero raises the batting average of the typical AL Roto team by .2747 - .2701 = .0046, as shown here:

	AB	H	BA
Average team with 13 hitters	5450	1472	0.2701
Vladimir Guerrero	549	176	0.3206
Average team with Guerrero	5999	1648	0.2747

To translate Guerrero's expected impact into SGPs in all four offensive categories, we simply divide his contribution by the SGP denominators:

Category	Guerrero's impact	AL SGP denominator	Expected SGPs
BA	0.0046	0.00182	.0046 / .00182 = 2.5
HR	34	9.5	34 / 9.5 = 3.6
RBI	113	29.6	113 / 29.6 = 3.8
SB	15	7.6	15 / 7.6 = 2.0
TOTAL			11.9

Tables 3-4 and 3-5 provide the expected 2006 stats of selected America League players, with SGP values calculated based on the equations above. These expected stats are based on the pre-season projections for these players published on the BaseballHQ.com web site. In some cases, these expected stats turned out to be an accurate estimate of the player's actual performance in 2006; in other cases, the player's season turned out quite differently than the forecast. As well as demonstrating the calculations involved, these tables will provide us with useful examples for later chapters.

Table 3-4

Hitters	Expected stats					Standings gain points				
	AB	BA	HR	RBI	SB	BA	HR	RBI	SB	TOT*
Rodriguez, A.	595	0.304	44	119	21	1.8	4.6	4.0	2.8	13.3
Guerrero, V.	549	0.321	34	113	15	2.5	3.6	3.8	2.0	11.9
Ortiz, D.	562	0.290	42	131	1	1.0	4.4	4.4	0.1	10.0
Suzuki, I.	637	0.305	12	60	32	2.0	1.3	2.0	4.2	9.5
Jeter, D.	619	0.304	18	68	16	1.9	1.9	2.3	2.1	8.2
Tejada, M.	638	0.288	24	100	6	1.0	2.5	3.4	0.8	7.7
Sizemore, G.	628	0.274	17	79	18	0.2	1.8	2.7	2.4	7.0
Mauer, J.	490	0.302	10	64	15	1.4	1.1	2.2	2.0	6.6
Ordonez, M.	529	0.297	19	83	1	1.3	2.0	2.8	0.1	6.2
Dye, J.	531	0.266	25	80	8	-0.2	2.6	2.7	1.1	6.2
Beltre, A.	604	0.260	25	93	5	-0.6	2.6	3.1	0.7	5.9
Granderson, C.	431	0.269	15	62	13	0.0	1.6	2.1	1.7	5.3
Morneau, J.	500	0.262	24	81	1	-0.4	2.5	2.7	0.1	5.0
Stewart, S.	568	0.283	10	60	8	0.7	1.1	2.0	1.1	4.8
Varitek, J.	453	0.276	18	70	2	0.2	1.9	2.4	0.3	4.8
Cano, R.	584	0.279	16	69	1	0.5	1.7	2.3	0.1	4.6
Guillen, C.	438	0.290	9	48	4	0.8	0.9	1.6	0.5	3.9
Catalanotto, F.	410	0.295	6	53	2	1.0	0.6	1.8	0.3	3.6
Derosa, M.	157	0.261	5	17	1	-0.1	0.5	0.6	0.1	1.1
Cora, A.	224	0.246	4	22	3	-0.5	0.4	0.7	0.4	1.0
Graffanino, T.	230	0.261	3	20	1	-0.2	0.3	0.7	0.1	0.9
Izturis, M.	133	0.241	1	10	6	-0.4	0.1	0.3	0.8	0.8
Bard, J.	123	0.244	3	13	0	-0.3	0.3	0.4	0.0	0.4
Branyan, R.	59	0.237	3	9	0	-0.2	0.3	0.3	0.0	0.4

*As a result of rounding, the Total SGPs may differ slightly from the apparent sum of the four preceding columns.

Table 3-5

Pitchers	Expected stats					Standings gain points				
	W	Sv	IP	ERA	WHIP	W	Sv	ERA	WHIP	TOT*
Santana, J.	19	0	218	2.81	1.03	5.6	0.0	3.4	4.5	13.5
Rivera, M.	5	43	73	2.34	1.00	1.5	6.8	1.7	1.9	11.9
Halladay, R.	15	0	203	3.06	1.11	4.4	0.0	2.6	3.1	10.2
Ryan, B.J.	3	36	73	2.96	1.08	0.9	5.7	1.2	1.4	9.2
Buehrle, M.	15	0	232	3.53	1.23	4.4	0.0	1.7	1.4	7.5
Beckett, J.	15	0	189	3.67	1.19	4.4	0.0	1.1	1.9	7.4
Radke, B.	11	0	203	3.99	1.20	3.2	0.0	0.4	1.8	5.4
Verlander, J.	4	0	116	3.03	1.05	1.2	0.0	1.7	2.4	5.3
Kazmir, S.	12	0	203	3.55	1.34	3.5	0.0	1.5	-0.3	4.7
Putz, J.J.	3	4	58	3.88	1.38	0.9	0.6	0.2	-0.3	1.4
Eaton, A.	6	0	87	4.45	1.36	1.8	0.0	-0.3	-0.3	1.2
Seanez, R.	4	0	58	4.81	1.28	1.2	0.0	-0.5	0.2	0.9
Carmona, F.	3	0	44	4.30	1.32	0.9	0.0	-0.1	0.0	0.8
Greinke, Z.	5	0	116	4.58	1.35	1.5	0.0	-0.6	-0.3	0.5

*As a result of rounding, the Total SGPs may differ slightly from the apparent sum of the four preceding columns.

Chapter 3 Postscript:
SGP Denominators for Non-standard Leagues

If your league is structured differently from the standard league, the SGP denominators recommended above may not accurately predict the amount of production required to move up one place in the final standings in a particular category. The important thing about SGP denominators is getting the relative values right for each category. If we were to double all of the denominators, our dollar values for players would not change at all. If we were to double the denominator only in the saves category, though, we would see closers plummet in value, while everyone else's dollar value would rise.

Therefore, if your league only differs from the standard league because, for instance, you have just 10 teams, then the SGP denominators provided above will probably work well.

Even though the final standings in each category are likely to be a little more spread out than these denominators would suggest, the change should affect each category about equally. The relative values for your league would probably remain consistent with these denominators.

If your league combines National and American League players, one alternative is to split the difference between the above denominators for each league. In RBIs, for example, the AL denominator is 29.6 and the NL denominator is 27.3, so use 28.45. You can also split the difference for the expected league average values in batting average, ERA, and WHIP.

However, much rests on the size of the mixed league. A 10-team league would have a higher concentration of talent than an 18-team league, and thus, a potentially different set of SGP equations. Although the above denominators may not exactly predict the differences in the standings at the end of the season, they should be near enough in relative terms.

The most difficult problem arises if your league uses stat categories other than the eleven categories presented above. You should still be able to use the above values for the eight standard categories plus runs scored, pitcher strikeouts, and innings pitched, but you may be on your own in estimating SGP denominators for your league's other categories. And you face a challenging task, because data is not readily available for non-standard categories. If you are able, you can use previous years' standings from your own league, or you can surf the Internet and try to find stats for other leagues with the same non-standard categories. Otherwise, you will just have to take your best guess. You can take comfort, however, in the thought that you probably still have a better method for valuing production in those categories than any of your competitors.

(Note: See page 127 for an additional essay on SGPs for non-standard categories.)

CHAPTER FOUR
Marginal SGPs

Many valuation methods share the same basic mistake: They translate standings gain points directly into auction dollars. In other words, they consider the best 276 players in the league and add up the total SGPs of those players. Let's say that total — to keep the arithmetic simple — is 1040 SGPs. They simply divide the total by 3120, the number of dollars available in the standard auction (12 teams * $260/team). By this method, each SGP would be worth $3, and each $1 would buy one-third of a SGP. Vladimir Guerrero, expected in 2006 to produce 11.9 SGPs, would be worth $36, while Alex Cora, expected to produce 1 SGP, would be worth $3. We can call this approach "Total SGP Pricing."

This approach seems logical, since the point of the auction is to use dollars to buy SGPs, but the example just given already hints at why this approach is flawed. We expect Guerrero to produce about 12 times as many SGPs as Cora. But would Guerrero go for only 12 times as much in the auction? Not likely. Guerrero might very well go for $36, perhaps even more. Cora, on the other hand, would almost certainly go for $1. No sane owner would pay $3 for those stats. Total SGP Pricing just does not fit reality.

We can see why if we consider the auction from a completely different perspective. Suppose you entered your auction with the intention of spending no money. Instead of trying to get the best team you could for $260, you are going to try to get the best team for $0. Wait a second — that's not allowed. The rules say you have to spend at least $1 for each player. The closest you can come to spending no money would be to spend $23. Suppose, then, that you tried to get the best $23 team. You would end up with the worst 14 hitters (more or less) out of the 168 hitters acquired and the worst 9 pitchers (more or less) out of the 108 pitchers acquired.

You would also end up with a certain number of SGPs. At $3 for every 1 SGP, Total SGP Pricing predicts that you would end up with 7.7 SGPs. In reality, however, you would end up with a lot more than 7.7 SGPs. Why? Basically, because the 168th-best hitter is always going to go for $1, but that hitter is going to be worth more than 0.333 SGPs. In my pre-auction valuations for the AL in 2006, the 168th-best hitter was Maicer Izturis. With projected stats of .241-1-10-6, I had Izturis worth 0.8 SGPs. So if you spent only $14 for your hitters, you would end up with Maicer Izturis and 13 slightly better guys, worth a total of at least 11.2 SGPs (14 * 0.8).

To keep things simple, suppose that the 108th-best pitcher is also worth 0.8 SGPs. Your $9 pitching staff would contain 9 guys worth 0.8 SGPs or slightly more, for a total of at least 7.2 SGPs (9 * 0.8). Your $23 roster is worth a total of at least 18.4 SGPs (11.2 + 7.2). That's more than twice as much as the 7.7 SGPs you would expect from the Total SGP Pricing method.

Somehow, though, the $23 roster doesn't excite you very much. You're in this league to have fun, and you think you'll have a lot more fun if you spend the whole $260. Fine, I agree. But you *have* to spend the $23, and you *have* to acquire a certain number of SGPs in the process. Now, if you *choose* to spend the additional $237, you'll want to use it to get the most additional SGPs that you can.

Dividing dollars and SGPs into these two pools is the key to my method of pricing. Call the $23 your "baseline dollars" and the SGPs that you can get for $23 your "baseline SGPs." Call the additional $237 your "marginal dollars" and the additional SGPs that you'd like to get the "marginal SGPs." My pricing method, which I call **Marginal SGP Pricing**, asserts the following:

> Auction value is not determined by allocating total dollars to buy the total SGPs available, because everyone must spend their baseline dollars, and they must get baseline SGPs for their baseline dollars. In effect, these dollars are already spent and these SGPs are already on everyone's roster before the auction begins. Therefore, auction value is determined by allocating marginal dollars to buy the marginal SGPs available.

Let's expand on the example above. We've assumed that the 276 best players are worth a total of 1040 SGPs. Twelve owners have a total of \$3120 to spend on those 1040 SGPs. Using Total SGP Pricing, that makes each SGP worth \$3. But each team has to spend the 23 baseline dollars and gets the baseline of 18.4 SGPs (0.8 SGPs per player) for doing so. What you really want to figure out is how to spend the 237 marginal dollars to buy the most marginal SGPs. Twelve owners with 237 marginal dollars each makes a total of \$2844. The total pool of marginal SGPs available is 819.2 (1040 total SGPs − (276 players * 0.8 baseline SGPs per player)). Therefore, the marginal dollars available to spend on each marginal SGP equals \$3.47 (2844 dollars / 819.2 SGPs). Table 4-1 summarizes the differences between the Total SGP and Marginal SGP approaches to pricing.

Table 4-1

	Total SGP Pricing	Marginal SGP Pricing
Players to be acquired	276	276
SGPs available	1040	819.2
Dollars to spend	3120	2844
SGPs per dollar	0.333 SGPs = \$1	0.288 marg SGPs = \$1
Dollars per SGP	1 SGP = \$3	1 marg SGP = \$3.47

For any given player, you should be willing to spend \$1 for his baseline 0.8 SGPs, then an additional \$3.47 for each SGP above that. Therefore, a player expected to produce 0.8 total SGPs would be worth only \$1, but a player expected to produce 2.8 total SGPs would be worth \$7.94 (\$1 + (2 * \$3.47)).

Going back to Guerrero and Cora, let's reconsider their value using Marginal SGP Pricing. Guerrero is worth 11.9 total SGPs, or 0.8 baseline plus 11.1 marginal. You should be willing to pay \$1 for the baseline plus \$3.47 per marginal SGP. At \$3.47 apiece, his 11.1 marginal SGPs are worth \$38.52. Add in the \$1 for his baseline SGPs and Guerrero's total auction value comes to \$39.52. Cora, on the other hand, is worth only 0.2 marginal SGPs on top of his 0.8 baseline SGPs. Therefore, you should be willing to spend only \$1.69 for him in the auction. Those values seem much more consistent with the prices in a real-life auction.

These sample players provide a taste of how values calculated under Marginal SGP Pricing compare to values derived via the more conventional Total SGP Pricing. Marginal SGP Pricing recognizes that players barely good enough to get purchased, like Cora, are worth only $1 or slightly more. Total SGP Pricing would predict a higher value for these players because it fails to recognize that the SGPs produced by the worst players just aren't worth more than $1.

The dollars that Marginal SGP Pricing "saves" on the low-end players get shifted to the high-end players like Guerrero. That's because this method recognizes that marginal SGPs are more scarce than total SGPs (819.2 vs. 1040), and it allocates more dollars to players with higher levels of marginal SGPs.

To extend the example a bit further, consider Frank Catalanotto, who was expected to produce about one-third the SGPs of Guerrero. Catalanotto, with total SGPs of 3.6, would be worth $10.80 (3.6 * 3) under Total SGP Pricing or $10.72 (1 + (2.8 * 3.47)) under Marginal SGP Pricing. The calculation for Catalanotto demonstrates that, in the middle, dollar values remain about the same. It's at the *margins* — the high and low ends — that the effects of Marginal SGP Pricing are felt.

The next chapter describes how we can expand upon Marginal SGP Pricing to quantify one of the long-standing mysteries of Roto pricing: position scarcity.

Chapter 4 Postscript
Auction Inflation in Carryover Leagues

Throughout Part I of this book, we are assuming that teams cannot carry players over from one season to the next. One consequence of player carryover is so important, however, that I must address it before continuing my discussion of Marginal SGP Pricing. If your league allows player carryover, you will almost certainly observe inflation in player values at auction time. (Auction inflation has been thoroughly discussed by other Rotisserie analysts, and I am not adding anything new to the concept here.)

Auction inflation occurs because owners retain players at salaries that are clearly below their auction value; that is, they retain a Jorge Cantu at $1, a Jeremy Bonderman at $6, a Grady Sizemore at $12, and so on. In carryover leagues, the dollars available in the auction are reduced by the salaries of the frozen players, but the SGPs available are reduced even more, since these frozen players have more SGP value than their salaries represent. As a result, the ratio of dollars to marginal SGPs increases, raising the value of all the available players in the auction.

To extend the example above, suppose that the 276 best players in the league have a total marginal SGP value of 819.2. Now suppose that before the auction, the owners in your league have frozen a total of 96 players with salaries totaling $1200 and marginal SGP values totaling 450. Therefore, the remaining 180 players to be acquired will have a total marginal SGP value of only 369.2 (819.2 − 450), but team owners will have a total of 1740 marginal dollars to spend on them (1920 total dollars − 180 baseline dollars). As a result, the price of a marginal SGP will rise from $3.47 (2844 / 819.2) to $4.71 (1740 / 369.2).

As long as you use the appropriate values for marginal dollars and marginal SGPs available for the auction, taking into account the salaries and values of the players that have been frozen, then Marginal SGP Pricing will compute prices properly. The dollar values of the best players (180, in our example) available to fill the open roster slots should add up to the total dollars ($1920) available for the auction. Auction inflation of 15%-35% is not unusual in established Roto leagues.

CHAPTER FIVE

Position Scarcity

O ne of the major by-products of Marginal SGP Pricing is a method for valuing a player's ability to fill a roster position where talent is scarce, like catcher. Marginal SGP Pricing solves this problem by recognizing that different positions may have different baseline SGPs.

Perhaps it is easiest to introduce this concept by first looking at the two major groups of players: pitchers and position players. Once we forecast expected stats for all players and convert those stats into SGPs, we can create two lists: one ranking all pitchers according to their SGP values, and another ranking all position players according to their SGP values. In the ideal auction, the top 108 pitchers will be selected, and the SGP value of the 108th-best pitcher defines the baseline SGPs for all pitchers. Likewise, the top 168 position players will be purchased in the auction. The SGP value of the 168th-best hitter defines the baseline SGPs for that group. (For the moment, we'll ignore the position eligibility issue among position players, though we'll get to that shortly.)

Will these two baseline SGP values — one for pitchers and one for hitters — be the same? They might be, but there is no reason they must be, and they will almost surely be different. As I mentioned in the last chapter, I rated Maicer Izturis as the 168th-best hitter going into the 2006 AL auction with an SGP value of 0.8. On the pitching side, I had Rudy Seanez as the 108th-best pitcher with an SGP value of 0.9. Close, but not the same.

Consider what this means about the relative value of hitters and pitchers in Marginal SGP Pricing. If a hitter and a pitcher each have an SGP value of 10.0 (or any equal value), then the hitter will be worth slightly more. The hitter's marginal SGPs are 9.2 (10.0 − 0.8), while the pitcher's are 9.1 (10.0 − 0.9). A pitcher with a total SGP value of 10.1 would have the same auction value as a hitter worth 10.0 SGPs.

The analysis gets quite a bit more interesting when we apply it to hitters who qualify at different positions. As any experienced Roto owner knows, it will probably not be the 168 best hitters who get picked up in the auction. Because of position eligibility requirements, owners almost always have to acquire some hitters outside the top 168 to fill certain talent-poor positions. As a result, some other hitters at the bottom end of the top 168 are left off Roto rosters. A league of 12 owners will have to obtain the following mix of position players at the auction:

  24 catchers
  12 first basemen
  12 second basemen
  12 shortstops
  12 third basemen
  60 outfielders
  12 corner infielders who qualify at either first or third
  12 middle infielders who qualify at either second or short
  12 designated hitters or utility players who qualify at any
  non-pitching position.

In theory, there is no reason why the top 168 hitters couldn't meet all of these requirements, but in practice they almost never do. Major league teams place more emphasis on the defensive ability of their middle infielders and catchers. As a result, the group of 168 hitters with the highest SGP values will probably contain fewer than 24 catchers and may fall short of 36 middle infielders. The group will likely include more than 60 outfielders and more than 36 corner infielders.

If the group of 168 does not contain 24 catchers, then it is not appropriate to use the SGP value of the 168th-best hitter as the baseline SGP for catchers. Instead, we have to look at the SGP value of the 24th-best catcher, because that is the player we will end up with if we wait until the end of the auction and get the last catcher available.

In fact, we really need to divide the hitters into two groups. Just as we initially thought of pitchers and position players as two separate pools of players, now we have two sub-pools within the pool of 168 position players: 24 catchers and 144 non-catchers. In addition to considering the 24th-best catcher to get the baseline SGPs for the catcher sub-pool, we have to look at the 144th-best non-catcher to determine the baseline SGPs for the non-catcher sub-pool.

Continuing to use the 2006 A.L. as our example, the 24th-best catcher was Josh Bard, worth 0.4 SGPs. Bard was only the 205th-most valuable hitter overall, but he or an even less valuable catcher would have to be picked in this auction to fill up 24 catcher slots. The top 168 hitters overall contained only 16 catchers, leaving Maicer Izturis as the 152nd-best non-catcher. Sorry, Maicer. You and seven other position players had to be left off of Roto rosters to accommodate all of those catchers. The 144th-best non-catcher was Tony Graffanino, worth 0.9 SGPs, or about 0.1 SGPs more than Izturis.

This analysis therefore reveals that the baseline SGPs for catchers (0.4) were 0.5 SGPs less than the baseline SGPs for non-catchers (0.9). This difference has significant implications for the auction values. If a catcher and a non-catcher have the exact same expected stats and consequently the exact same total SGP value, the catcher will have a marginal SGP value 0.5 higher than the non-catcher. In that 2006 AL auction, I had each marginal SGP worth about $3.69, so the extra 0.5 marginal SGPs would be worth about $2 (actually $1.85).

To demonstrate: Suppose you had both Jason Varitek and Shannon Stewart at 4.8 expected total SGPs. Varitek was the regular catcher for the Red Sox, while Stewart has only qualified at outfield while playing with the Twins. Varitek's marginal SGP value would be 4.4 (4.8 − 0.4), while Stewart's would be only 3.9 (4.8 − 0.9). At $3.69 per marginal SGP, Varitek's auction value would be about $17, while Stewart's would be only about $15.

If you've always been comfortable with the idea of paying more for players at talent-poor positions, I hope you're thinking, "Great, now I have a way to figure out exactly how much extra to pay." On the other hand, you may be wondering, "Do you really expect me to pay $2 more for the exact same stats just because a guy can play catcher?" The answer is, yes, I do. Why? Because if you don't, you'll end up with a Josh Bard on your roster instead of a Tony Graffanino.

Separating hitters into catchers and non-catchers is the simplest way to differentiate by position, and in many leagues that separation may be sufficient. In principle, though, we could create four sub-pools: catchers, middle infielders, corner infielders, and outfielders. The sub-pools would not be clear-cut, though, for two reasons: 1) many hitters qualify at more than one position, and 2) any hitter from any position can go into a team's utility slot. (For simplicity's sake, I am ignoring the distinctions between first and third basemen and between second basemen and shortstops. Because of the 12 flexible corner infield slots and the 12 flexible middle infield slots, it is highly unlikely that those distinctions could come into play.)

Despite these complications, though, it may be helpful to create a third sub-pool, most likely if the top 144 non-catchers do not include 36 middle infielders. In that case, you would need three sub-pools: the top 24 catchers, the top 36 middle infielders, and the top 108 hitters who qualify only at OF, 1B, or 3B. Again, you would find the player in each sub-pool with the lowest SGP value, and that would become the baseline SGP value for that sub-pool.

We now have the solution to one of the long-standing riddles of Roto valuation. You will find a clear benefit by taking proper account of position scarcity in your auction. For a variety of reasons, most owners fail to value position scarcity properly, and catchers tend to go cheaply in most leagues. Some owners seem not to consider position scarcity at all, and some owners seem intent on spending $1 apiece on their catchers, not realizing that a $1 player here has less value than anywhere else. Other things being equal, they would be better off buying a $1 outfielder.

Significant opportunities can also arise if there happens to be a shortage at middle infield in your auction. While the scarcity at catcher is widely recognized, some owners won't realize it when a middle-infield value shortage crops up.

The astute reader may already be thinking about how position scarcity can change during the course of the auction. We'll discuss that in Chapter 8. But first we need to shoot down one of the prevalent myths about Rotisserie valuation.

CHAPTER SIX
Why "Riskiness" Does Not Reduce Player Value

Before we continue with our discussion of how to implement Marginal SGP Pricing, I think it's important to address one of the common misconceptions of Roto analysis. It is often claimed that certain players or types of players are worth less in the auction because they are more "risky" than other players. That is, owners should pay less for players who are less consistent, less reliable in terms of performance. I have often seen assertions like this used to explain why only about 30% of the dollars in a typical auction are spent on pitching.

This argument about riskiness makes no sense if you are using expected stats to produce your auction values. Expected stats already take into account all of the scenarios for a player and reflect the average outcome of all of those scenarios. If you've used the method correctly, the chance that a player will produce value below his expected stats is exactly offset by value that he might produce in excess of those stats.

Sure, some players, like starting pitchers or injury-prone hitters, are less reliable performers than others. But their expected stats should provide a balanced assessment of their likely production. Of course, you will not want to bid as high as the values suggested by the best-case stats for these players. That's why I use expected stats rather than best-case scenarios in the first place. If you use best-case scenarios, how can you possibly know how much to fudge your dollar values? If you use expected stats, there's no need to fudge; the possibility of a better or worse performance is already captured in each player's SGPs.

Still not convinced that you should fearlessly pay up to the dollar value of the expected stats for Kelvim Escobar or A. J. Burnett? How about Troy Glaus, Magglio Ordonez, or Richie Sexson? Perhaps thinking of it another way will help. Suppose that you could participate in 100 different Roto leagues this year. I know, even one league destroys any semblance of your remaining life... let's make it one league a year for the next 100 years. Over that large number of seasons, your luck would almost certainly even out. If you estimated expected stats properly, some of your teams would outperform your expectations and some would under-perform, but overall it should balance out.

If other owners backed away from paying the expected-stats dollar value for players they viewed as risky, you could snap up those players cheap and end up winning more than your fair share of leagues. Therefore, there is no reason to discount the value of those players. You just have to be willing to ride the ups and downs that come with them.

The argument I have just made applies given our two initial assumptions: no player transactions other than trades and no player carryover from season to season. In Part II we will remove those assumptions, and we will learn that uncertainty about a player's performance can actually increase that player's value. Perhaps the only scenario where an owner should avoid risky players is in a carryover league when a team enters the auction with a large advantage based on retaining under-priced players from the previous season. In that situation, risky players can hurt you a lot more than they can help you.

Having dispensed for now with the need to worry about the riskiness of each player, we can move on and talk about how you can use expected stats and Marginal SGP Pricing in a spreadsheet to prepare for your auction.

CHAPTER SEVEN

Implementing Marginal SGP Pricing in a Spreadsheet

To deal with the extensive data manipulation and calculation required by Marginal SGP Pricing, I recommend using spreadsheet software such as Microsoft Excel on a personal computer. In fact, once you have set up a spreadsheet to handle Marginal SGP Pricing, you will not have to concern yourself too much with the performance valuation process, and you can return your focus to forecasting expected stats for players.

Step 1: Entering Expected Stats

The first step is to enter expected stats for a few players, using a format much like the one in the table at the end of Chapter 3. We'll use AL hitters in this example:

	A	B	C	D	E	F	G	H
1	**Player**	**Team**	**AB**	**Hits**	**BA**	**HR**	**RBI**	**SB**
2	Adams	Tor	499	130	0.261	6	53	9
3	AndersonB	CWS	440	117	0.266	13	49	4
4	Baldelli	Tam	522	143	0.274	12	66	16
5	Barajas	Tex	419	107	0.255	19	61	0
6	Belliard	Cle	535	147	0.275	13	68	3

The letters in the top row and the numbers in the left column of this example are hypothetical column and row coordinates from the spreadsheet. Later on, when I lay out the formulas you'll need to perform calculations, I'll continue to use the column and row coordinates from this hypothetical spreadsheet. However, your column and row coordinates may be different from the ones in this sample. Keep that in mind when entering the formulas into your spreadsheet — use the coordinates for your spreadsheet, not mine.

Although the sample spreadsheet shows players listed alphabetically, I suggest sorting your spreadsheet by team, so that all of the players on each major league team are grouped together. Then you will be able to make sure that you have assigned a reasonable number of at-bats (and, on your pitchers' spreadsheet, innings pitched) across each team. A team may have five quality outfielders, for instance, but they cannot all get 550 at-bats unless two of them play other positions. You will find that forecasting the correct number of at-bats is often the most important aspect of evaluating a hitter's performance. You can save a step by entering your estimated at-bats and batting average, then programming the spreadsheet to calculate hits for you (hits = at-bats * average).

When you have completed the expected stats for all players, have the spreadsheet calculate the totals in each category. Are your forecasts for total HRs, RBIs, SBs, and batting average consistent with major league totals from past seasons? The totals in the counting categories (HRs, RBIs, SBs) should actually be a little lower than past major league totals, since some of these stats will be produced in the coming season by players who are not available in the auction (e.g., players who begin the season in the minors). If you see major inconsistencies in these areas (for instance, a home run total that's above past totals), you need to make some adjustments.

In batting average, the total for the 168 hitters who will be acquired should equal the league average value that you are using in the SGP calculation. At this point, you have not yet determined who these 168 hitters are — that will have to wait until you've calculated SGPs for all hitters — but in general your total batting average for all of the hitters in your spreadsheet should be about .001 to .003 below your league's batting average. Once you eliminate hitters who will not be acquired in the auction, the BA of the remaining 168 should be close to the league average value used to calculate SGPs.

Step 2: Entering Position Eligibility Data

In order to deal with position scarcity, you will need information about position eligibility in your spreadsheet.

This information is also very handy during the auction. Insert several columns into your hitters' spreadsheet and enter a '1' to signify that a player is eligible at a particular position:

	A	B	C	D	E	F	G	H	I	***
1	Player	Team	C	1B	2B	SS	3B	OF	AB	
2	Adams	Tor				1			499	
3	AndersonB	CWS						1	440	
4	Baldelli	Tam						1	522	
5	Barajas	Tex	1						419	
6	Belliard	Cle			1				535	

The column on the far right with "***" in the top row signifies that not all of the columns in the spreadsheet are shown here. I will be using this convention since the spreadsheets will have too many columns to fit on these pages.

Step 3: Entering SGP Denominators and Formulas

Now you are almost ready to calculate SGPs for each player. To do so, you will need the SGP denominator information presented in Chapter 3. You can enter this data at the bottom of the spreadsheet, below your list of players :

	A	B
250	HR denom	9.5
251	RBI denom	29.6
252	SB denom	7.6
253	Team hits	1472
254	Team at-bats	5450
255	Team BA	0.2701
256	BA denom	0.00182

Next you add some more columns to the right of each player for SGP calculations. The symbols "[f1]," "[f2]," and so on represent formulas, which are provided below.

	A	***	N	O	P	Q	R	S
1	Player		SB	BA SGP	HR SGP	RBI SGP	SB SGP	TOT SGP
2	Adams		9	[f1]	[f2]	[f3]	[f4]	[f5]

[f1] = ((($B$253 + J2) / ($B$254 + I2)) - $B$255) / $B$256
[f2] = L2 / $B$250
[f3] = M2 / $B$251
[f4] = N2 / $B$252
[f5] = O2 + P2 + Q2 + R2

These formulas make the same calculations that we made for Vladimir Guerrero in Chapter 3. They divide the player's expected stats by the SGP denominator in each category to derive the player's expected SGPs. The last formula simply adds up the four SGP values (one for each category) to determine the player's Total SGPs.

A couple of things about the formulas. First, as I mentioned above, the cell and row coordinates used here apply only to this sample spreadsheet. That is, the formula for home run SGPs refers to cell B250 because the sample spreadsheet places the home run SGP denominator in that cell. If your spreadsheet places the home run SGP denominator in a different cell, then use that cell's coordinates when you enter the formula.

Second, the "$" symbols in these formulas perform a critical function; they let the computer know that the location of this cell will be the same for all players. For the cell references without the "$," the coordinates will automatically change from player to player (as they should, since each player's stats are on a different row). If you enter these formulas properly, you only have to type them in once; then you can copy them to all of the other rows in the spreadsheet.

When you have entered all your formulas and expected stats, and the spreadsheet has run the formulas, the first few rows should look like this:

	A	***	N	O	P	Q	R	S
1	Player		SB	BA SGP	HR SGP	RBI SGP	SB SGP	TOT SGP
2	Adams		9	-0.4	0.6	1.8	1.2	3.2
3	AndersonB		4	-0.2	1.4	1.7	0.5	3.4
4	Baldelli		16	0.2	1.3	2.2	2.1	5.8
5	Barajas		0	-0.6	2.0	2.1	0.0	3.5
6	Belliard		3	0.2	1.4	2.3	0.4	4.3

Step 4: Calculating Marginal SGPs

Your spreadsheet now requires only two more columns: one for marginal SGPs and one for dollar values. Before you can fill in those columns, however, you will need to do some data manipulation. First, you must sort all of the players in descending order of total SGPs. If your league will acquire 168 hitters, you can look at the 168th hitter on the list to get an initial estimate of the baseline SGPs for hitters. (If your spreadsheet is set up exactly like the one in our example, the 168th-best hitter will appear on row 169, since the best hitter will appear on row 2.)

This value will serve as the baseline for hitters unless position scarcity is in effect. To determine if there is position scarcity, total up the number of players eligible at each position among the top 168 hitters. If you do not find enough players to fill the roster slots at each position, then you will have to create separate sub-pools and determine a baseline SGP value for each sub-pool, as discussed in Chapter 5.

You can enter the baseline SGP value(s) at the bottom of the spreadsheet, below your SGP denominator values. If you found no position scarcity, you have only one value to enter:

	A	B
260	Hitter base SGP	0.8

If you found catchers to be in scarce supply, then you should have two sub-pools of hitters, and you will have two values to enter:

	A	B
260	Catcher base SGP	0.4
261	Non-C base SGP	0.9

If you found position scarcity for both catchers and middle infielders, then you will need three baseline SGP values:

	A	B
260	Catcher base SGP	0.4
261	2B/SS base SGP	0.7
262	1B/3B/OF base SGP	1

Now you are ready to add the column for marginal SGPs:

	A	* * *	R	S	T
1	Player		SB SGP	TOT SGP	MRG SGP
2	Adams		1.2	3.2	[f6]

The formula in this column subtracts baseline SGPs from Total SGPs to yield Marginal SGPs. If you have no position scarcity, then the new formula is simple:

[f6] = S2 – $B$260

If you have position scarcity, then you will have to employ one or more "if " statements and use each player's position eligibility information to determine which baseline value should be used for that player. For position scarcity at catcher only, depending on what spreadsheet software you use, the formula may look like this:

[f6] = if(C2 = 1, S2 – $B$260, S2 – $B$261)

This formula says, in effect, that if the value in the cell indicating the player's eligibility at catcher is '1,' then use the baseline SGP value for catchers; otherwise use the value for non-catchers.

For position scarcity at both catcher and middle infield, the formula gets rather complicated:

[f6] = if(C2 = 1, S2 - $B$260, if(or(E2 = 1, F2 = 1),
S2 – $B$261, S2 - $B$262))

The first two parts of the formula are unchanged. They say that, if the player qualifies at catcher, then use the baseline SGP value for catchers. The third part, which defines what the program should do if the player is not a catcher, becomes another "if " statement. This "if " statement says, if the player is eligible at either second base or shortstop (or both), then use the baseline SGP value for middle infielders; otherwise use the value for corner infielders and outfielders. This formula should always contain the three baseline values in order from lowest to highest, so you may need to change it if, for example, middle infielders have a lower baseline than catchers in your league.

If you have scarcity at catcher only, and you have copied the correct formula down column T for all players, then a few selected rows of your spreadsheet may now look like this:

	A	* * *	R	S	T
1	Player		SB SGP	TOT SGP	MRG SGP
2	Adams		1.2	3.2	2.3
3	AndersonB		0.5	3.4	2.5
4	Baldelli		2.1	5.8	4.9
5	Barajas		0.0	3.5	3.1
* * *					
10	ChavezE		0.9	6.9	6.0

At this point, you can sort all hitters again in descending order of marginal SGPs, and you can check two things to ensure that your marginal SGP values are correct. First, the 168th-best hitter should have marginal SGPs of zero. Second, if you want to check that you have adjusted properly for position scarcity, you should now have a sufficient number of players at each position among your top 168 hitters. In fact, you should have exactly the minimum number of players needed at any scarce position (for instance, 24 catchers). If you now have more than the minimum, you have over-adjusted for position scarcity.

Step 5: Converting Marginal SGPs into Dollar Values

The final step is to convert these marginal SGP values to dollar values. To do this, you need to know the total marginal dollars and the total marginal SGPs available in your auction. The total marginal dollars equal the total dollars all teams have for the auction minus the total number of players to be acquired. In a standard league, this value is 3120 − 276 = 2844. To calculate the marginal SGPs available, you need to have completed all of the steps up to this point for hitters and pitchers. Then you can total the marginal SGPs of the top 168 hitters and top 108 pitchers to determine the total available in the auction. These values go in two more cells at the bottom of the spreadsheet:

	A	B
265	Marg $$$ in auction	2844
266	Marg SGP in auction	770

(If your league allows player carryover, enter the values in these two cells for the marginal dollars and marginal SGPs actually available in your auction, taking into account the players that are retained on rosters from the previous season. As we discussed in the Chapter 4 Postscript, entering these values will adjust your dollar values to reflect auction inflation.)

The final formula in your spreadsheet goes into a column at the far right:

	A	* * *	R	S	T	U
1	Player		SB SGP	TOT SGP	MRG SGP	$$$ VAL
2	Adams		1.2	3.2	2.3	[f7]

[f7] = 1 + (T2 * ($B$265 / $B$266))

The '1' in this formula represents the baseline dollar that is part of every player's value. The rest of the formula converts the player's marginal SGPs to marginal dollars. In this example, each marginal SGP is worth $3.69, reflecting the ratio of the total available marginal dollars to marginal SGPs. When this formula has been calculated for all players, your spreadsheet should now look like this:

	A	***	R	S	T	U
1	Player		SB SGP	TOT SGP	MRG SGP	$$$ VAL
2	Adams		1.2	3.2	2.3	9.3
3	AndersonB		0.5	3.4	2.5	10.1
4	Baldelli		2.1	5.8	4.9	19.0
5	Barajas		0.0	3.5	3.1	12.4
***						
10	Chavez		0.9	6.9	6.0	23.2

The SGP values as shown here are rounded to the nearest tenth, which is why some dollar values appear inconsistent with the displayed marginal SGPs. For example, Adams' 2.3 marginal SGPs would seem to be worth 1 + (2.3 * $3.69) = $9.5, but the spreadsheet will contain a value of 2.26 for his marginal SGPs, producing the result 1 + (2.26 * $3.69) = $9.3.

Step 6: Creating a Spreadsheet for Pitchers

The process for pitchers is completely analogous to that for hitters except that you need not worry about position eligibility or position scarcity. The expected stats portion of the spreadsheet might look like this:

	A	B	C	D	E	F	G	H	I
1	Player	Team	W	Sv	IP	ER	ERA	H+BB	WHIP
2	Bedard	Bal	11	0	174	72	3.72	242	1.39
3	Blanton	Oak	13	0	203	78	3.46	235	1.16
4	Bonderman	Det	14	0	189	86	4.10	244	1.29
5	Contreras	CWS	13	0	189	81	3.86	241	1.28
6	CorderoF	Tex	3	41	73	25	3.08	90	1.23

The hazards of predicting pitcher performance are evident in these examples from the start of the 2006 season. I prefer to input innings pitched, ERA, and WHIP information and let the spreadsheet calculate the ER and H+BB columns. You may prefer to input hits plus walks, perhaps even as separate numbers, and let the spreadsheet calculate WHIP.

You will need the following data at the bottom of the spreadsheet for the SGP, marginal SGP, and dollar value calculations:

	A	B
250	W denom	3.4
251	Sv denom	6.3
252	Team IP	1050
253	Team ER	484.2
254	Team ERA	4.15
255	ERA denom	0.067
256	Team H+BB	1386
257	Team WHIP	1.32
258	WHIP denom	0.011
259		
260	Pitcher base SGP	0.9
* * *		
265	Marg $$$ in auction	2844
266	Marg SGP in auction	770

The formula section of the pitchers' spreadsheet will look like the following:

	A	* * *	I	J	K	L	M	N	O	P
1	Player		WHIP	Win SGP	Save SGP	ERA SGP	WHIP SGP	TOT SGP	MRG SGP	$$$ VAL
2	Bedard		1.39	[f1]	[f2]	[f3]	[f4]	[f5]	[f6]	[f7]

[f1] = C2 / $B$250
[f2] = D2 / $B$251
[f3] = ($B$254 - (($B$253 + F2) / (($B$252 + E2) / 9)))
    / $B$255
[f4] = ($B$257 - (($B$256 + H2) / ($B$252 + E2))) / $B$258
[f5] = J2 + K2 + L2 + M2
[f6] = N2 - $B$260
[f7] = 1 + (O2 * ($B$265/$B$266))

Once you have completed all of this work, you will have a very powerful tool for analyzing and manipulating player values. You can change any player's statistics and see how his dollar value changes. You can also change the values used to calculate SGP denominators and see how that affects dollar values. Think that these SGP denominators are placing too much value on steals? Just increase the stolen base denominator from 7.6 to a higher value and watch everyone's steals become less valuable. Remember that if you do make significant changes to the denominators, you may need to recalculate your baseline values and the marginal SGPs available.

These spreadsheets are very handy during the auction itself. In addition to bringing a complete copy of each to the auction, I like to sort the hitters' spreadsheet by position so I have a ranked list of the hitters available at each position.

In the next chapter, we will talk further about how to use these spreadsheets and values in the auction. We will discuss why you may want to make an additional upward adjustment to the baselines. With the spreadsheets, you can easily do so and recalculate dollar values.

Chapter 7 Postscript:
Why the 70/30 Hitter/Pitcher Split?

The actual results of hundreds of Roto auctions indicate that, on average, leagues have historically allocated their cash about 70/30 between hitting and pitching. Roto analysts have struggled to explain why this should be so. Some have suggested that the shortfall of spending on pitchers is due to the fact that pitchers are riskier investments, so owners spend less on them. We showed in Chapter 6 why that explanation does not make sense.

Alex Patton has asserted that, since the aggregate value of the rate categories must be zero, there are only five categories that have positive aggregate value. Three of these (HRs, RBIs, and SBs) are hitting categories, while only two (wins and saves) are pitching categories. Therefore, Patton says, hitters should comprise 60% of the total value in the auction and pitchers the remaining 40%. He has wrestled with explanations for the 10% difference between his theory and reality.

I believe that Patton erred when he assumed that all five of the counting categories should have equal total value.

There is no reason why the total SGPs in, for example, the saves category should equal those in home runs. In fact, they do not. In a typical league, the last-place team may have 100 or more HRs. This last-place total may represent ten or more SGPs of value, and all of the other teams will naturally have greater value. (By definition, the average 11th place team will have one more SGP of value than the last place team, the average 10th place team will have one more than the 11th place team, and so on.)

In saves, though, the last place team may be in the single digits. This team's last-place total may represent only one or two SGPs of value. So the total SGP value of all saves will be much lower than the total for homers. This indirectly reflects the fact that most saves are bunched in only about 15-20 pitchers in a league, whereas home runs are widely distributed among hitters.

When you have completed your valuation spreadsheet, you can sum up each SGP column to ascertain the total SGP value of the available hitters and pitchers in each category. You should see that the total value in HRs is much greater than the total value in saves. As an additional check on your overall calculations, you should see that hitters make up about 65-70% of the total dollar value, with pitchers accounting for about 30-35%.

CHAPTER EIGHT

Dynamics of the Auction

Y our objective in the auction is to fill your 23-man roster with the most valuable set of players possible. To accomplish that, you must spend your $260 to acquire much more than $260 worth of player value. Ideally, you will purchase each of your 23 players for less than he is worth on your spreadsheets.

Whenever a player is nominated, you should immediately refer to the appropriate spreadsheet to remind yourself of the dollar value you calculated. As the bidding approaches that dollar value, your chances of reaping a "profit" (i.e., stats that are worth more than what you paid for them) decrease. How close to this dollar value should you bid? Experienced owners develop intuition about what constitutes an acceptable profit. The best formal method I know of to help you make this decision is called "optimal bidding." It was developed by John Benson and is described in his book *Rotisserie Baseball: Playing for Blood.*

Based on experience and observation of many auctions, Benson has calculated how much of a player's dollar value you should pay. This percentage varies substantially among different types of players. For instance, for "everyday hitters," Benson says you should bid 65%-75% of the dollar value. For "injury rehab pitchers," the optimal bidding range is 35%-45%. Obviously, very few players will be available at these kind of discounts, but, says Benson, if you stick to these levels throughout the auction, you should find enough bargains to fill up your roster.

In theory, you should only worry about getting maximum value on your roster, regardless of what form that value takes. If everyone else is paying too much for pitchers and under-spending on hitters, then you should take the best bargains on hitters and buy whatever pitching is left over. You can always make trades after the auction to correct any imbalances on your roster. As long as you are able to make fair-value exchanges in the trades, the advantage you establish by accumulating the most player value at the auction should give your team the edge throughout the season. (Admittedly, making what you consider to be fair-value exchanges may prove quite difficult in practice. I discuss this problem in Chapter 17.)

Adjusting Player Values During the Auction

In developing our values for each player, we make a number of major assumptions. We assume that other owners will pay close to fair value for each player. We assume they will not acquire players who are not among the best 168 hitters and the best 108 pitchers. We assume they will not purchase extra players at positions where talent is scarce.

In a real auction, other owners will almost certainly violate all of these assumptions. Some of their violations will have a significant effect on our values, others may not. In any case, it is well worth reviewing the possible effects, so that you can recognize them as they arise and judge for yourself whether or not they are significant.

Violation #1:Overpaying or underpaying for players.

Suppose that other owners purchase players for prices significantly different from the values you had projected. That's what Roto is about, after all. Different owners have different expectations for the same players. Occasionally, other owners will stop bidding on a player at a level well below your value. In that case, you should usually buy the player (unless, of course, you don't have a slot available or don't have enough dollars left). Much more often, especially early in the auction, other owners will bid above your value. Of the 11 other owners, a couple are bound to have higher expectations for the player than you do.

Every time a player goes for a price different from the value you projected, the values of all other remaining players change slightly. Recall that we are allocating marginal dollars to buy marginal SGPs; the ratio of marginal dollars to marginal SGPs defines the value of each marginal SGP. If a player goes for more or less than you projected, the ratio of remaining marginal dollars to marginal SGPs changes slightly, so the values of all remaining players change as a result.

Let's take an example using the numbers from last chapter's sample spreadsheet. We start off with a pool of 770 marginal SGPs and 2844 marginal dollars. At the outset, then, each marginal SGP is worth \$3.69 (2844 / 770). Alex Rodriguez, worth 12.4 marginal SGPs, has an initial dollar value of \$46.76 (\$1 + (12.4 * \$3.69)). Now suppose that the first player auctioned off is David Ortiz. You think Ortiz is worth 9.1 marginal SGPs, or \$34.58 (\$1 + (9.1 * \$3.69)). But a couple of other owners love Ortiz, and he goes for \$44. Now the value of all remaining marginal SGPs have decreased. There are only 2801 marginal dollars left to buy the remaining 760.9 units of value, so each marginal SGP is now worth only \$3.68 (2801 / 760.9). Rodriguez' value has dropped 13 cents, to \$46.63 (\$1 + (12.4 * \$3.68)), and the value of all other remaining players has dropped proportionally. As you can see, the effect of a single overpriced player is negligible, but as these small changes accrue over the course of an auction, the overall effect can become quite significant.

I use the same method other analysts have described to adjust values as the auction progresses: I keep a running "overpayment tally" of the cumulative amount my competitors have overpaid for players. If the first player bid on goes for \$44 and I had him worth only \$35, then I write down "9," because the player went for \$9 too much. If the next player is sold at \$34 and I had him valued at \$29, I scratch out the "9" and write "14," adding \$5 to the total amount that has been overpaid. If I think the third player is worth \$26 and am able to buy him for \$23, then I scratch out the "14" and write "11," because the total overpayment has dropped by \$3. I have seen the overpayment tally get up to \$200 or more by the end of the auction.

Keeping track of the total amount overpaid allows you to calculate a "deflation factor" for the remaining players in the auction. To calculate the deflation factor, you need to know both the total overpayment and, at least approximately, how many total marginal dollars remain to be spent. The total marginal dollars remaining (TMDR) is the amount all owners have left to spend minus the number of roster spots they have to fill. It's nice to know this number exactly, although you will probably have more critical things to keep track of. If you can estimate TMDR within 100, you'll be close enough. The deflation factor is then simply:

Deflation factor = TMDR / (TMDR + overpayment tally)

For instance, if your overpayment tally has reached 150, and 1350 marginal dollars remain in the auction, then the deflation factor equals 1350 / (1350 + 150), or 1350 / 1500, which is 0.9, or 90%. You started with 2844 total marginal dollars, and you allocated a total of 2844 marginal dollars of value among players. Now 1494 marginal dollars have been spent, but owners have purchased only $1344 of value. As a result, 1350 marginal dollars are now chasing $1500 worth of value. So you should now be able to buy players for $0.90 on the marginal $1.00. (Note that if the overpayment tally is negative, the deflation factor will exceed 1 and will actually be an inflation factor.)

Technically, the deflation factor only affects the marginal dollars of each player's value. The first dollar of each player's value remains worth $1, because we have to spend a dollar for every player. However, this subtlety only makes a few cents' difference, and in the heat of the auction it's not worth the trouble to factor it in. Just multiply a player's dollar value by the deflation factor; you'll get a good estimate of his adjusted value.

In my experience, the deflation factor may well fall below 90% midway through an auction. In the very late stages, it may plummet to a much lower value. At that point, though, only cheap players will be left, and the deflation will be manifest in $4 players being bought for $2.

By the way, this deflation is completely analogous to auction inflation as discussed in the Chapter 4 Postscript. In this case, however, owners are typically overpaying for players, rather than underpaying, as they do when they choose to carry over players from the previous season. The adjustment we make for deflation during the draft is effectively the same as the calculation for auction inflation.

Violation #2:Acquiring players outside the best available

Other owners will also violate your assumptions by purchasing players that you considered to be outside the pool of the best 276 players. In my experience, this is much more likely to happen with pitchers than with hitters, particularly with starting pitchers, so in our examples below we will assume it happens with a pitcher. This error on the part of your competitors (at least, we hope it's their error) has two effects on your player valuations.

First, to the extent that they pay more than $1 for the player, they remove marginal dollars from the pool without removing marginal SGPs. In this respect, the purchase contributes to deflation, just as any other overpayment does. In updating your overpayment tally, however, you should assume that the value of the player purchased was $1, not whatever lesser value you actually assigned to the player.

The second, and more important, effect of this player purchase is that it redefines the baseline SGPs for all remaining pitchers. Because another owner has filled one of his or her roster spots with a pitcher outside your pool of the best 108 available, you know that you will now be able to get a slightly better pitcher if you buy the last pitcher available in the draft. Before the auction, you assumed that if you bought the last pitcher available with your last $1, then you would get the 108th-best pitcher; now you can get the 107th-best pitcher with your last $1. Therefore, the SGPs of the 107th-best pitcher become your new baseline SGPs for all remaining pitchers. (If the player was a hitter, then this effect would apply to all other hitters in the same position subpool.)

This second effect also reduces the total marginal SGPs remaining in the auction. Because the 107th-best pitcher has slightly more SGPs than the 108th-best, a slightly larger baseline number is now being subtracted from the SGPs of all remaining players at the affected position(s). Therefore, the marginal SGPs for each of those players will decline slightly.

The precise effects on player values depend on the situation. In general, we can say that the dollar values of remaining players at the affected position(s) will decline in absolute terms, and they will also decline in relation to the value of players at positions that were not affected. That is, if a pitcher outside the top 108 is selected, then the value of all pitchers (the affected group) falls in relation to the value of hitters (the unaffected group). We cannot say for sure whether the values of players at unaffected positions will increase or decrease. The net effect will depend on how many marginal dollars were spent, which will tend to decrease the value of all players, and on the change in baseline SGPs at the affected position(s), which will tend to increase the value of players at unaffected positions.

How on earth does one adjust for these effects in the course of an auction? If there is an easy method, I have not yet discovered it. My suggestion is to try to anticipate these effects when producing your values before the auction. In other words, adjust the baseline SGP ahead of time to the level where you think it is likely to end up. This requires some guesswork. You know that the other owners will not be in complete agreement with you as to exactly who the 276 best available players are. If you end up acquiring the last pitcher, you will surely get someone better than #108 on your list — but how much better? As I said, guesswork. To some extent, the answer will depend on the quality of your competition. The better the other owners in your league are, the less likely they are to pick players outside your top 276.

Based on my own experience, I can suggest some very rough guidelines. Of your top 168 hitters, the best one not selected in the auction (that is, the best one you could end up picking to fill your last spot) will probably fall between #150 and #160. Therefore, you might want to use the SGP of your 155th-best hitter for your baseline. If you have sub-pools of hitters based on position scarcity, then use a number of similar proportions for each sub-pool — that is, a number about 90-95% of the way down the list. For instance, in a sub-pool of 24 catchers, using the SGP of the 22nd-best as the baseline would probably be about right. For pitchers, there will be much greater disagreement among owners. The best pitcher available at the end of the auction will probably not be anywhere near #108 on your list; he may fall anywhere between #70 and #90.

As a general rule, it's a good idea to be conservative in making this adjustment — that is, you should err on the side of making the adjustment too small. When other owners acquire players not among your top 276, they are sending the implicit message that you don't know who the top 276 players really are. Your list may be completely right, or theirs may be completely right, but the truth is probably somewhere in between. So if 20 of your best 276 players go unselected, don't be smug; it probably means that about 10 of those players weren't that good to begin with.

Violation #3: Purchasing extra players at scarce positions.

Suppose you determine that talent is scarce at catcher (as is usually the case). You create two sub-pools among the hitters, 24 catchers and 144 non-catchers. Now suppose that during the auction an owner who already has two catchers purchases a third from among your top 24 catchers. Perhaps he is placing the third catcher in his utility slot, or perhaps one of the three qualifies at another position. To avoid making the example more complicated, we will assume he pays your estimated dollar value for the player.

You now know that one additional catcher will have to be purchased in the auction, making a total of 25. At the same time, only 143 non-catchers will be purchased. This changes the baseline SGP for both sub-pools, lowering the baseline for catchers to the SGP value of the 25th-best catcher and raising the baseline for non-catchers to the SGP value of the 143rd-best non-catcher. This will increase the value of the remaining catchers relative to the remaining non-catchers. In addition, the dollar value of marginal SGPs will change for all players, since the total remaining marginal SGPs will change. We cannot say for sure whether that total will increase or decrease; in this example it will probably decrease, making each remaining marginal SGP slightly more valuable.

As with Violation #2, there is no easy way to adjust values

when this happens during the auction. The occurrences are rare enough and the effects small enough that you probably shouldn't worry about making adjustments. This violation will probably not happen more than a couple of times in the typical auction, and the resulting changes in baseline values are likely to be small.

The most important reason to discuss Violation #3, however, is to make sure that you do not commit this violation yourself without fully understanding the implications. Remember, players at talent-scarce positions are worth more because if you do not spend marginal dollars at that position, you will have to accept especially weak players to fill those roster spots. The 24th-best catcher will not produce as many SGPs as the 144th-best non-catcher. As soon as you have bought two catchers, though, you are no longer comparing catchers to the 24th-best catcher. A third catcher would have to go at a position where non-catchers qualify. From now on, you are comparing catchers to non-catchers; as far as you are concerned, there are no longer separate sub-pools. The remaining catchers should now be valued on the same baseline as non-catchers.

If you recognize position scarcity and value it properly, you will likely be one of the most aggressive bidders for players at scarce positions. Therefore, it is especially important to remember that, once you have filled that position, those players should no longer command a scarcity premium from you (although they still should from owners who have not filled that position). In effect, you need to revert to values using the baseline for the hitters at non-scarce positions. You may even want to include a column of such values on your spreadsheet so you have them available when the time comes.

There is so much else to keep track of during an auction that it's virtually impossible to adjust your player values every time an owner commits one of the three violations described in this chapter. Someday we may have a computer program that can make precise alterations during the auction. Until that day arrives, all you can do is make rough adjustments — which still puts you a leg up on your competitors.

Chapter 8 Postscript: More Notes on the 70/30 Split

As we discussed in the postscript to Chapter 7, in most Roto auctions about 70% of the dollars are spent on hitting while only 30% are spent on pitching. In that postscript, I offered one explanation for the strong bias toward hitting.

I believe we stumbled upon a further explanation in our discussion of Violation #2. If the auction conformed perfectly to our assumptions, dollars would be allocated among hitters and pitchers according to our original pre-auction dollar values. But the auction never does conform to our assumptions, particularly among pitchers. Disagreement over the value of pitchers is much greater than disagreement over the value of hitters. Almost all of our top 168 hitters will be purchased, but a much smaller proportion of our top 108 pitchers will be. As a result, we have to raise our baseline for pitchers by a larger amount than we do for hitters. The net effect of this is a shift of value from pitchers to hitters.

To illustrate with an example (and to keep the arithmetic simple): Suppose we go into an auction with 1000 marginal SGPs, 650 for hitters and 350 for pitchers. During the auction, we raise the baselines by 0.5 for hitters and 1.0 for pitchers to adjust for cases of Violation #2. On the hitting side, we have reduced the total marginal SGP by 84 (168 hitters * 0.5). On the pitching side, we've reduced the total by 108 (108 pitchers * 1.0). We now have only 808 total marginal SGP, 566 for hitters and 242 for pitchers. On a percentage basis, the hitter/pitcher split has shifted from 65/35 to about 70/30.

The riskiness of pitchers may indirectly cause this shift, but the true cause is the disagreement among owners about the value of pitchers. If everybody knew that pitchers' performances would vary a great deal from their expected stats but all owners agreed about what those expected stats were, then we would not observe the shift in value from pitchers to hitters. But since expected stats for a given pitcher vary so much from owner to owner, lists of the top 108 pitchers also vary. As a result, we see the shift in value from pitchers to hitters.

Overall, everybody gets marginal SGPs cheap for pitchers because we cannot agree on where those marginal SGPs are.

CHAPTER NINE

The Rest of the Season

O nce you have completed your draft, the rest of the season begins. So far, we have been operating under the assumption that you can make trades but cannot otherwise pick up or drop players (remember, in Part II we'll drop this assumption). You can use the concepts of SGPs and SGP denominators to evaluate trade possibilities throughout the season. And the principles described below will continue to hold true when we consider other transactions in addition to trades.

After the auction, total SGPs replace marginal SGPs as the key measure of a player's value. During the auction, when every player has a baseline value of $1, we must focus on marginal SGPs, but for the rest of the season we can simply look at a player's total SGP value. In analyzing a possible trade, you need not distinguish between the baseline and marginal SGPs of the players involved. You need only compare total SGPs and try to swing deals where you are acquiring more total SGPs than you are trading away.

If during the auction you strictly pursue the goal of obtaining maximum value, you will likely end up with an unbalanced team — you'll have more SGPs than you need in some categories and fewer than you need in others. As soon as the draft is over, you should seek trades to redress this imbalance.

Initially, you may have trouble finding willing counterparts for your trades. If the other owners were bidding up certain types of players in the auction, they will probably not be quick to trade those players soon afterward. Once the standings begin to sort themselves out, however, and your rivals recognize that they need what you have, the trade opportunities should begin to materialize. You should try to take advantage of these opportunities sooner rather than later, especially if the imbalances on your team are substantial. Otherwise, you will fall farther and farther behind in your weak categories, with less and less time to close the gap.

As the season progresses, expected stats for individual players change constantly. Obviously, you will revise your forecasts for most players as their situation changes throughout the season. In some cases, the change will be dramatic, as when a player is seriously injured, moves from the bench to a regular role, or raises his game to a new level (Justin Morneau was a prime example in 2006). In other cases, a player may simply perform at a slightly higher or lower level than expected, and the change will be subtle. An owner should constantly reassess his own players, as well as any players he might acquire in a trade, to determine whether their expected stats, and consequently their SGP values, have changed.

SGP denominators for the league also will change during the season, as the races in certain categories become tighter or more spread out. In the first couple of months, these changes can be difficult to determine. Even if it appears that the race in a category is tightening or spreading out, circumstances can change with unexpected developments for individual players and trades by other owners. By midseason, though, the situation in each category will start to become clearer. The value of players who contribute in the close categories will increase as you revise the SGP denominators for those categories downward.

Late in the season, the value of SGP denominators may differ substantially from team to team. In the draft and the early stages of the season, we should think of the SGP denominators as being the same for all teams. As the standings start to sort themselves out in the second half, however, one team may be battling several others in a tight race in a particular category, while another team finds itself well behind the team above it and comfortably ahead of the team below. In effect, these two teams now have different SGP denominators for the same category. The denominator for the first team has gotten much smaller, and players who can help in that category have become very valuable to the team.

For the second team, by contrast, the denominator for the

category has gotten much larger, and the same players are not worth much at all. This situation naturally suggests a trade between the two teams. If they are in the reverse situation in another category, they can easily make a deal that will benefit both owners.

If you are comfortably in first place or hopelessly in last place in a category, extra SGPs have no value at all. A team that finishes in first place in a category gets the maximum number of points from that category, regardless of its margin of victory. If your team is headed for a clear first place finish in a category, you should be aggressively trying to trade your extra SGP value in that category. The SGP denominator in the category has gotten very large for you. The same reasoning holds if you are on course to finish last in a category. If you can acquire enough additional SGPs in that category to move out of last place, you should consider doing so. If not, then you should trade away as much of the value you have in that category as possible. An easy first place finish in a category and a close last place finish are both signs of poor roster management.

PART TWO

Option-Adjusted Marginal SGP Pricing

CHAPTER TEN
Introducing Options

Throughout Part I, we stuck to two assumptions:

Assumption #1: Other than trades, no player transactions during the season. No players can be added to active rosters from reserve rosters or the free agent pool.

Assumption #2: No player carryover to next year. Next season, you start with a clean slate.

Now we are ready to remove those assumptions. And it's about time. Probably 99% of Roto leagues allow transactions during the season and/or carryover of players from year to year.

When Glen Waggoner and his Roto colleagues published the first edition of *Rotisserie League Baseball* in 1984, their "Official Constitution" only allowed an owner to remove a player from his or her active roster when that player was removed from the active roster of his major league team. When they published their 1989 third edition, however, Waggoner et al. unveiled a new version of the rules, named "Rotisserie Ultra," that permitted owners to remove players from their active rosters and replace them at will.

The "Ultra rules," as I will refer to them henceforth, also called for a reserve draft after the completion of the auction draft. In this reserve draft, owners simply take turns selecting players who were not purchased in the auction. Each owner thereby creates his or her reserve roster, a set of players the owner controls, but whose stats do not count unless the owner makes a subsequent transaction to promote a player to the team's active roster.

Most leagues have since adopted some form of this freedom to remove a player at any time from the active roster and replace him with a player from the free agent pool or reserve roster. In addition, many leagues also allow owners to retain some players on their rosters over the winter and into the following season. Under the official rules, both original and Ultra, an owner can keep a player at the same salary for up to two years after the season in which he was acquired in the auction. If the owner wishes to sign the player to a long-term contract, he can keep the player for even longer.

The ability to drop and add players during the season and to retain players for the following season(s) gives each owner a set of options. These options have value and thus affect the overall value of players in the auction and during the season. In this chapter, I will introduce the subject of options and try to help you to develop some intuition about option value. In the rest of Part II, I will examine how to value the various Roto options and how to take these option values into account in Roto decision-making.

* * *

Options have played an increasingly important role in finance since the opening of the world's first formal options market, the Chicago Board Options Exchange, in 1973. An option is a contract that gives its holder the right to buy or sell something at a specified price by a certain time in the future. An option that gives its holder the right to buy is a "call" option, while an option that gives its holder the right to sell is a "put" option. To use an example from the financial world, an investor might hold a call option on stock in the XYZ Corporation. This option gives the investor the right to buy one share of XYZ stock from the person who sold him the option. To complete the definition of the option, we need to know 1) how long the investor has this right, and 2) at what price the option allows the investor to buy the one share. Perhaps the option allows the investor to buy one share of XYZ stock for $50 at any time during the next three months. The $50 price set by the option is referred to as the option's "exercise price."

Both types of options play a role in Rotisserie. A call option gives an owner the right to activate or retain a player; a put gives its holder the right to remove a player from his roster.

Consider this example. If you paid $6 for Danny Haren in 2005, you got Haren on your team for that year. You also got the right to keep Haren the next year at the same price. And if you exercised that right, then you would also have the right to keep him on your team for the 2007 season, again at $6. You would even have the right to sign him to a long-term contract in the spring of 2007, allowing you to keep him through 2008 or beyond at a higher price.

So when you buy a player in the auction, you acquire not only that player's services for the current season but also a series of call options on that player for future seasons. In this context, the use of the term "option" may already be familiar to baseball fans, since the term is used to describe similar arrangements in real-life major-league player contracts.

Call Options

Returning to the aforementioned XYZ $50 call, does this option have value to our hypothetical investor? Should he be willing to pay something for it? Remember, by buying the option the investor doesn't acquire the stock; he simply gets the right to buy stock. If he exercises the option, he still has to pay for the stock itself. Why should he pay for the mere right to pay for something else?

In this case, if XYZ is currently trading in the stock market at a price higher than $50, then the option obviously has value; the investor could exercise his option to buy XYZ stock for $50, then sell it for a higher price, making an immediate profit. If XYZ stock is trading in the market for $60, the investor can make an immediate $10 profit by exercising his call and selling stock for the market price.

The amount that can be gained by immediately exercising an option is referred to as the option's "intrinsic value." For a call option, intrinsic value equals the stock price minus the exercise price (e.g., $60 - 50 = 10$). Assuming the option can be exercised immediately, it will always be worth at least as much as its intrinsic value.

An option can be worth something even if its intrinsic value is zero. Suppose, to continue our example, that XYZ stock is now trading at $50. Should our investor be willing to pay something for a call option that lets him buy one share of XYZ stock for $50 anytime in the next three months? If the stock price never goes above $50, the option will be worthless, but if the stock does trade higher, the option will have some intrinsic value at that time. The value of holding that option today depends on two things: how likely it is that XYZ stock will trade above $50 in the next three months, and how much above $50 it is likely to trade. The more likely the stock is to trade at a higher price, the more the option will be worth.

An option's value can never be negative. It does the investor no harm if he simply holds the option and never exercises it. If there is absolutely no chance that XYZ stock will trade above $50, then the call option will have zero value. If there is any chance at all, however, then he should be willing to pay something for that possible opportunity today.

Essentially, the calculation of an option's value boils down to an expected value calculation, just like the calculations we do to determine expected stats. (Remember the example of Johan Santana's wins back in Chapter 1?) Table 10-1 contains a sample probability distribution of XYZ stock prices and associated call option values.

Table 10-1

XYZ stock price	Probability	Value of call option with exercise price of $50
$45	25%	$0
$50	50%	$0
$55	25%	$5
	Net value=	$1.25

In this example, there is a 50% chance that XYZ will stay at $50, its current price. The stock also has a 25% chance of dropping to $45 and a 25% chance of rising to $55. Only in the last case will the call option have any value. In that scenario, it will be worth $5 ($55 stock price - $50 exercise price). Since that scenario will only arise 25% of the time, the value of the option before we know the outcome of the stock price will be 0.25 * $5 = $1.25.

Now consider another stock with the probability distribution of prices shown in Table 10-2.

Table 10-2

ABC stock price	Probability	Value of call option with exercise price of $50
$40	25%	$0
$50	50%	$0
$60	25%	$10
	Net value=	$2.50

This example is quite similar to the one involving XYZ stock except that the price of ABC stock is more volatile. Notice what happens to the call option price with the more volatile stock — even though ABC stock is also currently trading at $50, the option value has doubled simply because ABC is more volatile than XYZ. The possibility that the stock will drop all the way to $40 does not hurt the value of the call option — it's worth zero no matter how far below $50 the stock drops. However, because it's more likely that the stock price will rise above its current price, the call is worth more.

In other words, an increase in the volatility of the stock can only increase the value of an option on that stock. When we start examining Roto options, we will find that, for the same reason, the most valuable options are on players whose performance is highly uncertain.

Put Options

Having taken a quick look at calls, let's turn to the second type of options — puts. A $50 put on XYZ gives its holder the right to sell one share at $50. You can think of a put option as an insurance policy; no matter how low XYZ stock goes, the holder of this option will still be able to sell it at $50. The intrinsic value of a put option equals the exercise price minus the stock price. Like a call, a put option has, at worst, zero value. If there is some chance that the stock will trade below $50, then the put will have some positive value. In Table 10-3, we return to our sample price distribution for XYZ stock to compute a value for this put.

Table 10-3

XYZ stock price	Probability	Value of put option with exercise price of $50
$45	25%	$5
$50	50%	$0
$55	25%	$0
	Net value=	$1.25

Put options play a less critical role in Rotisserie than call options but an important role nevertheless. The primary form of a put option in Roto is the right to get rid of a player who is performing poorly. This option is particularly important for pitchers, who can really hurt a team if they start producing high ERA and WHIP numbers.

The more valuable put options only exist if you're playing under Rotisserie Ultra rules. Under the original Rotisserie rules, an owner cannot remove a player from his roster unless that player is removed from his major league team's active roster. In other words, if a player stinks but stays on the major league roster, there's nothing his Roto owner can do about it unless he can find some sucker who will take the player in a trade. Owners have only very limited put options on their players under the original Roto rules.

Under the Ultra rules, owners hold put options on all players; they can replace anybody at almost any time. And in certain cases they are — or should be — willing to pay for that option. If you have played Roto by the original rules and by the Ultra rules, then you may have noticed the effect that put options can have on auction prices.

In Ultra, owners are more likely to take a chance on marginal starting pitchers, pitchers they wouldn't touch if the original rules were in force. Consider someone like Vicente Padilla, who had a down year for the Phillies in 2005, compiling a 4.71 ERA and 1.50 WHIP for only 9 wins in 147 IP. Padilla moved to the Rangers in 2006, and in leagues playing by the original rules, visions of Padilla pitching as he did in 2005 for six long months in Texas' hitter-friendly ballpark probably kept most owners from bidding even $1 on him in the 2006 auction. But with the addition of a put option under Ultra rules, Padilla's value increased; the knowledge that he could be deactivated if he got off to a horrendous start made owners more apt to risk a few dollars on him.

Options are a difficult subject to understand. Professionals in the financial markets spend years honing their ability to value options. The concepts will become clearer as we apply them to Roto and consider various examples. If you're an experienced Roto owner, you've probably had some common-sense understanding of these concepts all along. Now you'll be learning a method that will allow you to apply the concepts more consistently and analytically.

CHAPTER ELEVEN

Options to Retain Players in Future Seasons

I f your league allows you to carry over some players from one season to the next — as the official Rotisserie League Baseball rules prescribe — then you and the other owners in your league have an important set of call options to consider. These call options give you the right to retain players on your roster for future seasons. This type of option, which I refer to as a "future-season call option," has more potential than any other type to affect player values, both on auction day and during the season.

Any experienced Roto owner appreciates the value of having a dramatically under-priced player on his roster. Maybe you took a chance on Joe Nathan at the start of the 2004 season, when the Twins' bullpen situation was unclear, and Nathan was a mere spring training contender to collect some regular season saves. Suppose you valued Nathan using Marginal SGP Pricing and concluded that his expected stats for 2004 were worth $5. Further suppose that you were, in fact, able to buy Nathan for $5 in your auction. By midseason, Nathan was clearly established as the Twins' closer, and he was suddenly much more valuable than any comparable but fairly priced closer, say a $40 Mariano Rivera.

If we just look at 2004 performance, Nathan was not more valuable than Rivera. Yet Nathan clearly had greater future value as a $5 keeper for 2005. This fact would have been evident on the trade market. Nathan at $5 would have brought much more than Rivera at $40 in a trade, because other owners would have recognized Nathan's future value. You could have exchanged Nathan's value in future seasons for value that would have helped you win in the current year; that is, you could have traded your options on Nathan.

Quantifying potential future value is vital for pricing players in the auction, as well as for assessing player value in midseason when considering trades. We can quantify this value by regarding the opportunity to retain under-priced players in future seasons as a call option and using options theory to come up with a value for the option.

Actually, if a player is currently in the first year of his contract, we have a set of call options to retain that player. We have an option to keep him on our roster next year at his current salary. If we exercise that option, then we will have two additional options the following spring: to renew the player's contract at the same salary for a final year or sign him to a long-term contract. For now, to keep things simple, we will consider only the option to keep the player next year.

Whether or not we keep the player next spring depends on whether, at that time, his expected dollar value in the auction exceeds his current salary. If it does not, we release the player back into the player pool. Even if we like the player, it does not make sense to keep him at his current salary if we expect to be able to buy him for less in the auction.

If the player's expected auction price exceeds his salary, then we exercise our call option and keep him on our roster (or we may trade him to another owner who wants to keep him). The value of the call option at that time will be the difference between his expected salary and his actual salary. For instance, if, when the spring of 2005 rolls around, we expect Joe Nathan to go for $35 in the auction, then our option to keep him at a $5 salary is worth $30. We can use the $30 we save on Nathan to buy other players.

Valuing the option at the time of exercise is straightforward and simple. Valuing it ahead of time is more complicated but also more important. We are trying to estimate what the option will be worth a year from now, when we will have to decide whether or not to keep the player on our roster. To estimate the expected value of the option, we first have to estimate what the player's value will be. The process is analogous to estimating the probability distribution of stock price values as in the last chapter and to estimating expected stats as described in Chapter 1.

Placing a Value on Future-Season Call Options

At the time of the 2004 auction, one might have projected the probability of Joe Nathan's value for the next year's auction as shown in Table 11-1. To simplify, we round all values to the nearest $5. (Throughout our discussion of future-season call options, I will refer to dollar values rather than SGPs, although the two are interchangeable; we could just as well express player values and exercise prices in terms of SGPs. Because the exercise price of the future-season call — the player's salary — is already expressed in dollars, though, I will stick to that measure in this analysis.)

Table 11-1

Nathan's value in next year's auction	Probability	Value of option to keep Nathan at $5
$0 or less	25%	$0
$5	35%	$0
$10	13%	$5
$15	8%	$10
$20	8%	$15
$25	5%	$20
$30	3%	$25
$35 or more	3%	$30

Estimating a 60% chance that Nathan would be worth $0-5 in the 2005 auction may seem harsh, but remember that we're assuming these forecasts were made in the spring of 2004. At that time, there were challengers for the closer's role in Minnesota. Nathan had been an effective set-up man the year before for the San Francisco Giants, but that was in a different league, and Nathan had failed to convert several save opportunities that year. There were all types of scenarios under which Nathan might have been worth just a few dollars in the 2005 auction. The other probabilities reflect the likelihood that Nathan would increase his value over the next year by establishing himself as a premier set-up man or possibly winning a closer's job.

To calculate the expected value of the option at next year's auction, we multiply the probability of each outcome by the corresponding option value, then add the products together:

**(0.25 * \$0) + (0.35 * \$0) + (0.13 * \$5) + (0.08 * \$10)
+ (0.08 * \$15) + (0.05 * \$20) + (0.03 * \$25) + (0.03 * \$30)
= \$5.30.**

An expected option value of \$5.30 might seem high, but it actually ended up being worth about \$30! If you paid \$5 for Nathan simply because you thought his pitching would be worth \$5 in 2004, you got quite a bit of hidden value in the form of this call option.

If we ended our analysis here, these calculations would suggest that Nathan, with an expected 2004 performance worth \$5 and a future season call-option worth \$5.30, should be worth \$10.30 in the auction. Unfortunately, the calculation gets a bit more complicated. First, we must consider that, with each additional dollar we pay for Nathan, the exercise price of the option increases, making the option less valuable. If we were to pay \$10 for Nathan, then the positive option values at each level of performance would decrease, as shown in Table 11-2.

Table 11-2

Nathan's value in next year's auction	Probability	Value of option to keep Nathan at \$10
\$0 or less	25%	\$0
\$5	35%	\$0
\$10	13%	\$0
\$15	8%	\$5
\$20	8%	\$10
\$25	5%	\$15
\$30	3%	\$20
\$35 or more	3%	\$25

The total value of the option would decrease accordingly:

$$(0.25 * \$0) + (0.35 * \$0) + (0.13 * \$0) + (0.08 * \$5)$$
$$+ (0.08 * \$10) + (0.05 * \$15) + (0.03 * \$20) + (0.03 * \$25)$$
$$= \$3.30.$$

Paying \$10 for \$5 worth of 2004 performance and a \$3.30 option would not make much sense.

Second, we have to consider that a payoff in the future — in this case, one year in the future — is always worth less than a payoff in the present. We should pay less than \$5.30 today for something that will be worth \$5.30 in one year. And third, remember that whatever value we assign to Nathan for the 2004 auction — whether that value is based on his expected current-year performance or on his future-season call option — we still have a fixed pool of \$3,120 to allocate. Though options can increase individual player values, they cannot increase the total value available in the auction.

We'll address these issues one at a time. In this chapter, we will walk through the basic option calculation and the expected value of these options. In the next chapter, we will discuss the issue of future value versus present value. And in Chapter 14, we will talk about how to put all of these considerations together and modify your spreadsheet to ensure that your option-adjusted values add up to \$3,120.

To persuade you that this extra effort will be worth your while, let me say a few words about the benefits we derive by adding options to our analysis of player values. Option-adjusted valuation gives us the most precise analysis of the value of any particular player, enabling us to quantify the "hidden" value of future potential and weigh it against present value. When key decisions arise concerning a specific player — how much to bid on him in the auction, how much to ask for in a trade, whether or not to sign the player to a long-term contract — we will have the ability to do better analysis and make a better decision.

I will offer some shortcut methods for how to apply options theory to make consistent adjustments to the values of all the players in your auction. Though only approximate, these adjustments should give you a significant edge over rivals who fail to appreciate the importance of option-adjusted values.

With that motivation in mind, let us forge ahead, building on our Joe Nathan example. Nathan's high option value at the start of 2004 is based on our assessment that his auction price might be dramatically higher in 2005 than in 2004. This assessment is based, in turn, on Nathan's capabilities as a pitcher, especially his strikeout dominance (83 Ks in 79 IP in 2003), and on the unsettled state of the Twins' bullpen. In this sense, valuing call options still depends on baseball knowledge and forecasting ability, just as Marginal SGP Pricing depends on accurate expected statistics.

Compare Nathan to another relief pitcher with the same expected 2004 value, $5, but without a realistic opportunity to become a closer. Oakland's Chad Bradford had capitalized on his unusual delivery to establish himself as an effective middle reliever. Likely to pick up a few relief wins and maybe a save or two, Bradford figured to be worth a few bucks. But Bradford clearly had the pitching repertoire and skill set of a capable middle-innings guy. The chances were negligible that he would become a closer and command a $25+ price in the next year's auction. The $5 call option on Bradford therefore had far less value than the option on Nathan.

As we saw when we increased Nathan's current salary from $5 to $10, the value of the call option will decrease fairly quickly as the player's salary — the exercise price of the call — increases. For this reason, call options are not likely to be worth much on established players with salaries of $20 or higher. Sure, occasionally a player in this category will unexpectedly raise his game to a higher level, but this sort of improvement happens so infrequently — its probability is so low — that there is rarely a reason to attach significant option value to such players. Of course, if you have some reason to believe that a specific established player is about to have a breakthrough season, then, by all means, add option value to that player. In general, however, the most valuable future-season call options apply to younger, developing players who are available at lower salaries.

Because a player must increase sharply in value within one year (or, at most, two) for an owner to reap the value of his call option, certain types of developing players will tend to have the highest option values. Players with outstanding base-stealing ability and pitchers with the potential to be closers are two prime examples. If given the opportunity to steal bases or save games regularly, these players can quickly rack up SGPs. Opportunity, by the way, can be just as important as ability in determining whether a player achieves his upside potential within the one- or two-year time frame. If a talented player has an established veteran ahead of him in the organization, your option may expire worthless. Beware of assigning too much option value to the following types of highly-touted prospects:

1. Starting pitchers with no major league experience. They rarely become successful in the majors without at least a year or two of seasoning. (Roy Halladay went 18-17 with an ERA of 4.95 in parts of four seasons before becoming a top-flight starter.)

2. Catchers and middle infielders, who are often regarded as great prospects because of their defensive ability but have little to offer Roto owners. The best glove men are sometimes rushed to the majors before they are really ready to face major league pitchers.

3. Star prospects who spent the previous season in the low minors (A ball and below) and are available in the reserve draft. Although there are spectacular exceptions like Miguel Cabrera and Albert Pujols, these players are usually too far from the majors to warrant even a reserve pick.

Recognizing Option Value During the Auction

The final portion of the auction, when most of the remaining players are going for $1, is an especially important time to be aware of call-option values. At this point, you are likely to be choosing among, on the one hand, established part-time players who can be counted on to provide limited value every year, and, on the other hand, prospects who may get little playing time this year (or may even go back to the minors) but have great potential for the future. As with stocks, options on baseball players whose value is highly volatile are worth more than options on players whose value is stable. Usually, you should seize the opportunity to acquire an option with an exercise price of $1 on a young prospect. The option value for a promising prospect will ordinarily outweigh any small difference in expected current-season performance between the young player and a veteran bench player.

Call-option values are also critical when considering which players to select in the reserve draft. The whole purpose of the reserve draft is to acquire the best portfolio of call options on players who may become valuable in the future. Some players will be appealing due to their potential to increase in value during the current season. (We will discuss that type of call option in Chapter 13.) Others will be good reserve selections because of the value of their future-season call options.

The players available in the reserve draft fall into one of two categories: 1) players of so little value that they were not among the 276 players acquired in the auction, and 2) players not eligible for the auction, which in many Roto leagues includes minor leaguers.

The second group will contain many players with valuable future-season call options. Players picked in the reserve draft effectively have salaries of zero for the current season, but, according to the Ultra rules, if they are retained for the following season their salaries will vary from $15 to $2, depending on the reserve round in which they were selected. The Ultra rules also allow an owner to retain on his reserve roster up to three players from the reserve draft of a previous season, if those players are major league rookies and have never been active in his Roto league. Such a player has an effective salary of zero for the following season. Therefore, his future-season call option will have an exercise price of zero, which can make the option quite valuable.

Let's look back on one player who, if you picked him in your 2005 reserve draft, was eligible to be frozen on your reserve roster at the start of 2006. That player was Ian Kinsler, who in 2004 split the year between A (.402-11-52-16 in 59 games) and AA (.300-9-46-7 in 71 games) in the Texas Rangers farm system. You might, in the spring of 2005, have estimated Kinsler's future value as shown in Table 11-3.

Table 11-3

Kinsler's value in next year's (2006) auction	Probability	Value of option to keep Kinsler at $0
$0 or less	65%	$0
$5	18%	$5
$10	8%	$10
$15	5%	$15
$20	3%	$20
$25 or more	1%	$25

At the time, Kinsler did not appear likely to be on an American League roster by the spring of 2006, especially not with a regular playing opportunity. But the possibility did exist; with evident power skills to go along with some speed, Kinsler clearly had strong potential. If he were to play well in 2005, the option to freeze him on a reserve roster in 2006 (assuming he remained a rookie) could become quite valuable. Based on the above distribution estimated in the spring of 2005, that option would be worth

(0.65 * $0) + (0.18 * $5) + (0.08 * $10) + (0.05 * $15) + (0.03 * $20) + (0.01 * $25) = $3.30

As it turned out, after a promising 2005 in AAA (.274-23-94-19), Kinsler won the second base job in Texas in early 2006, making the option on him valuable indeed. A typical auction price for Kinsler was about $12 in 2006, so the option ended up being worth about $12 ($12 intrinsic value − $0 exercise price). Of course, Kinsler ended up being one of the top-hitting second basemen in the AL that year.

CHAPTER TWELVE
Applying a Discount Factor to Future Seasons

As mentioned in the last chapter, $1 that you will have at some time in the future, say one year from now, is not worth as much as $1 you have today. From a financial perspective, if you have $1 today, you can put that money in the bank or somewhere else where it will earn interest, and you will have more than $1 when one year has gone by. In financial terminology, if you are to receive a payment of $1 in one year, that payment has a "future value" of $1, but it has a "present value" of less than $1. You have to determine an appropriate "discount factor" to calculate its present value.

In the last chapter, when we discussed call options to retain Joe Nathan or Ian Kinsler in the following season, we calculated what those options were expected to be worth one year in the future. To help us convert that future value to a present value that we can use for this year's auction, we need to determine an appropriate discount factor.

Broadly speaking, discount factors consist of two components. The first component is the risk-free interest rate, and the second component is a risk premium over the risk-free rate. In finance, the risk-free interest rate is the rate at which money is borrowed and lent when the loan is certain to be repaid. Officially, the interest rate on US government securities is considered to be the risk-free rate, but you can think of the rate on your money market account as being about equal to the risk-free rate. Although this rate fluctuates over time, a typical risk-free interest rate is about 5%.

The second component of the discount factor, the risk premium over the risk-free rate, reflects the possibility that money lent out might not be repaid. Those in the business of lending out money, like banks or loan sharks, charge lower interest if they feel almost certain to be paid back and higher interest if they are not so certain. Why charge higher interest when repayment is uncertain? Because those borrowers who do pay back have to make up for those who do not. What we have, then, is another expected value problem in disguise.

When we apply this thinking to Roto, the issue isn't whether the other owners in your league are going to pay up. Instead, we need to consider whether your league is going to take place at all next season and whether you will continue to own a team in it. All of those valuable call options for next year's auction will not be worth anything to you if your league disbands over the winter or if you drop out for any reason. At times, we have even had to worry about whether there would be major league baseball next season.

You may think it's a sure thing that your league will last through next year, but there is always some chance that, for one reason or another, it will not. Or, perhaps some of the same owners will have a league, but you have to start the season without carrying over any players, which will have the same effect on your call options. Even for an established, stable league, I would suggest that the probability that the league will be around a year later is not higher than 80-90%. For a new league or a league that has high turnover and must scramble for new owners every spring, the probability may be much lower. The lower this probability, the less those options in future seasons are worth today.

The equation for an appropriate discount factor for your league, then, is...

$$D = P * (1 / (1 + r))$$

...where "D" is the discount factor you are calculating, "P" is the probability that your league will take place next year, and "r" is the risk-free rate. P and r are both expressed as a fraction of one (that is, an 85% probability is expressed as 0.85 and a 5% risk-free rate is expressed as 0.05). D must fall somewhere between 0 and 1. If you want to make the equation even simpler, you can use $D = P * (1 - r)$, which will produce nearly the same discount factor as long as r is not too large.

A discount factor of about 0.8 (80%) is reasonable for an established, stable league, based on a risk-free rate of about

5% and a P-value of about 85%. Again, for less stable leagues, the discount factor may be much lower. We will apply the discount factor to options for future seasons when we expand our pricing spreadsheet in Chapter 14.

All option values for next season should be discounted by D. For instance, with a discount factor of 0.8, an option expected to be worth $5 next year would have a value today of 0.8 * $5 = $4. If your discount factor is only 0.5, then the option would have a present value of only 0.5 * $5 = $2.50.

If you are discounting a value from two years in the future, you must multiply by the discount factor twice. With a discount factor of 0.8, the present value of an option expected to be worth $5 in the auction two years hence would be 0.8 * 0.8 * $5 = $3.20. (You could have a different discount factor for the second and subsequent years, if you think that the value for P or r is significantly different in a later year.)

The uncertainty captured by the discount factor should not be confused with uncertainty applying to specific players; it should apply consistently for all players in the league. For instance, you should not say to yourself, "I'm not so sure about this option on Nathan. He might get hurt and miss the season altogether. I think I better lower the discount factor for him." If you have doubts of this sort, then you should be adjusting the probability distribution for Nathan's expected future value. You should not, however, modify your discount factor to reflect uncertainty about individual players.

You may want to adjust your discount factor for one other reason, though. As we have calculated the discount factor so far, we have assumed that you have no particular preference for winning your league this year over next year. In fact, owners often do have such a preference. If you have a strong team and feel you have an excellent opportunity to win your league this year, you may not want to compromise that opportunity to improve your team for next year. In this case you may want to lower your discount factor for next year substantially, maybe even to zero. If you lower your discount factor to zero, then you will place no value on options for future seasons.

Other owners may find themselves in just the opposite situation, especially as the season progresses. They may conclude that they have no chance to win this year and therefore only care about the future value of players. Those owners effectively put a discount factor of zero on a player's value for the current season and consider only the player's future value. The result, of course, is the bane of Rotisserie: dumping trades, where an owner who is in contention trades away players with valuable future-season call options to a team that is out of the pennant race. In exchange, the contending owner receives players with little future-season call option value but plenty of expected value in the current season.

Undoubtedly, you understood dumping trades before you understood discount factors, but now you have another way of looking at them.

CHAPTER THIRTEEN

Options to Activate and Drop Players During the Season

Options to retain players in future seasons tend to be the most valuable Roto options, but the option to activate or drop a player during the current season can also be quite important. Under the Ultra rules, each owner has two sets of options within a given Rotisserie season. First, an owner has a put option on each player on his active roster, the ability to remove a player from his roster at almost any time. I refer to this type of option as a "current-season put option." Second, he also has a "current-season call option" on each player on his reserve roster, as well as a possible current-season call option on each player in the free agent pool. He can activate these players at almost any time. (Under the original Roto rules, which allow much less flexibility to activate and drop players, calls and puts play a minimal part in valuing players.)

Players' performance levels, and consequently their SGP values, change constantly during the season. Most often these changes are simply the result of unexpectedly strong or weak production, but changes in value can also result from injuries, trades, and other events that expand or constrict a player's role on his team. To succeed, a Roto owner must recognize these changes and make appropriate roster moves. Options theory is useful both in assembling a roster on auction day that will be conducive to in-season maneuvering and in making the best decisions about moves during the season.

Intrinsic Value of Current-Season Call Options

In many ways, the reasoning we developed for future-season calls in Chapter 11 applies directly to current-season options, but there are a couple of significant differences. One straightforward difference is that we need not discount current-season options, since their value is not that far in the future and not subject to the risk of whether our league has future seasons. A more complex difference arises when we try to determine the exercise price on our options.

For future-season call options on a particular player, the exercise price is the player's salary, but what is the exercise price of a call option to activate a player during the season?

Suppose that you selected the Orioles' Nick Markakis during the 2006 reserve draft. Markakis, a 22-year-old outfielder with decent gap power, had a good spring training, unexpectedly earning a reserve spot in a crowded Baltimore outfield alongside the 33-year-old David Newhan. Newhan breaks his leg in late April, while Markakis keeps hitting, earning himself more and more starts until he is a full-time player in mid-May. Before the season, your expected stats for Markakis reflected the low probability of his getting a chance to play. But now, in late May, that probability has risen to 100%. You come up with a new expected stats forecast for Markakis at that point, figuring he will now get about 400 more at-bats, and you decide that his expected production for the remainder of the season will be 2.0 SGPs.

However, the value of exercising your call option to activate Markakis will be less than 2.0 SGPs. You have a limited number of roster spots, and Markakis will have to take the place of another player; when you activate him, you will simultaneously have to reserve or waive somebody and give up that player's expected production. I refer to that other player as the "alternative active player," the player who would be active if Markakis were not.

Therefore, the exercise price of your call option on Markakis — or on any player you activate — will be equal to the value of the alternative active player. And the value of the call option when you exercise it will equal the difference between the value of the player you are activating and value of the alternative active player.

At first glance, it might seem that the value of the alternative active player could vary tremendously. For example, you might have another outfielder on your active roster who just got injured (maybe you even have Newhan), in which case the exercise price of your call on Markakis would appear to be zero — you're not losing any production by reserving the injured player. Conversely, perhaps you already have five good outfielders, plus a good hitter in your utility slot. Maybe you expect all six of those players to be worth at least 2.0 SGPs for the rest of the season. In that case, the exercise price of your option would appear to be at least 2.0, and the value of the option (Markakis' value minus the alternative active player's) would be negative. You would not even want to activate Markakis.

Assuming, though, that you can call up free agents and make trades, this evaluation of the alternative active player, and hence of the exercise price, is misleading. In the first scenario, in which one of your active outfielders just got injured (i.e., has zero value), the alternative to Markakis is not really zero. If you did not have Markakis, you could replace the injured outfielder with the best outfielder available in the free agent pool or on your reserve list. This hypothetical alternative player would be some baseline-quality outfielder with about the same value as the 168th-best hitter in the league. Therefore, the real alternative to Markakis is not a player with zero value but rather a player worth about as much as the least valuable hitter on any active roster in your league. (Let's forget about position scarcity for the moment.)

Similarly, under the second scenario, in which you are loaded with outfielders, the option on Markakis clearly still has positive value. In this situation, any good Roto owner would trade an outfielder to benefit from Markakis's increased value. You might trade one of your outfielders to another owner who has a shortage at that position (perhaps to Newhan's owner) and get back a good hitter who plays, say, shortstop. Or you might get a good pitcher. To make room for whatever player you acquire, you would deactivate a (presumably) poorer player at the corresponding position. Therefore, rather than replacing one of your outfielders, Markakis in effect takes the roster spot of a weak player at another position.

The point is that, in general, the exercise price on a call option will always be roughly equal to the value of a baseline player. If you do not have a baseline-type player on your roster, other owners will, and you can realize the value of your option by trading. So the value of the 168th-best hitter in the league approximately determines the exercise price for current-season call options on hitters, just as he determines the baseline SGP level for the auction. If position scarcity is in effect, then the value of the baseline hitter in the appropriate sub-pool would establish the exercise price. For pitchers, the value of the 108th-best hurler sets the exercise price.

Baseline SGP values will decrease as the time remaining in the season decreases. You can use the baseline SGP values you determined at auction time and simply pro-rate them for the time remaining in the season to estimate the current exercise price of an option. If the baseline SGP value for non-catchers was 0.9 on auction day, then at the end of May, with two-thirds of the season remaining, the exercise price of options on non-catchers would be 0.9 * 2/3, or about 0.6 SGPs. Your call option on Markakis would then be worth 1.4 SGPs, the difference between his expected production of 2.0 SGPs and the 0.6 SGPs of the baseline player.

Future Value of Current-Season Call Options

The Markakis example demonstrates how to calculate the value of a current-season call option at the time of exercise. To estimate the future value of a current-season call — that is, a call that we may want to exercise at some point during the season — we need to do an expected value calculation. Remember, current-season call options are only applicable to players who are not on an active roster (or, before the auction, players who are not expected to be on an active roster). Players who have an expected SGP value above the baseline value will probably start the season on an active roster and thus will not have a current-season call option. Current-season call-option value will apply only for players whose expected value falls below the baseline.

For any such player, we must consider how likely it is that

at some point in the season his value will rise above the baseline, and by how much it might rise above. The value of the call option on a player is the average of those possible values.

Let's return to Markakis' situation but backtrack to the beginning of the season. Suppose that, at the time of the auction, you expected Markakis to be worth 0.8 SGPs (leaving him just outside the pool of non-catchers expected to be purchased in the auction, since the baseline for that group was 0.9 SGPs). Your forecast was based on three scenarios:

1. With 30% probability, he would spend almost the entire season in the minors and would not produce any SGPs.

2. With 50% probability, he would get about 160 ABs and produce 0.8 SGPs.

3. With 20% probability, he would get about 400 ABs and produce 2.0 SGPs.

These scenarios are consistent with your forecast of 0.8 SGPs: $(0.30 * 0.0) + (0.50 * 0.8) + (0.20 * 2.0) = 0.8$.

In scenario 1, you would not activate Markakis, and the call option would be worthless. In scenario 2, you might activate him, since he would be nearly equivalent to the baseline player, but the option still would not have any value, since Markakis' value would be about the same as the alternative active player. In scenario 3, you would surely activate Markakis, and, assuming the activation takes place at a point in the season when the exercise price (baseline value) is 0.6, then the call option would be worth $2.0 - 0.6 = 1.4$ SGPs. Since the third scenario will only occur 20% of the time, the value of this option at the start of the season would be 20% of 1.4, or 0.28 SGPs.

As we discussed with future-season call options, if two players have the same expected SGP value, the one with the greater upside potential will have greater current-season call option value. Here we will compare Markakis to Todd Hollandsworth. Because he has moderate power and can pinch hit, Hollandsworth can be counted on for about 200 ABs a year, but he has very little chance of getting more playing time at this stage of his career. In the event of an injury to another outfielder, his team would probably give a promising rookie a shot at the job. With a high degree of certainty, we could expect Hollandsworth to be worth about 0.8 SGPs in the 2006 season, no matter what happens.

What is the value of the call option on Hollandsworth? Close to zero. Since he will probably never be worth much more than the baseline player, we will probably never want to activate him. Even though Hollandsworth has the same expected production as Markakis (0.8 SGPs), Hollandsworth's current-season call option has almost no value while Markakis' has some. Once again, in low-value players, riskiness (i.e. volatility) actually makes players more valuable. The probability that Markakis will produce less than Hollandsworth does not hurt his value, because we would not expect either player to be active anyhow. But if Markakis realizes his upside potential, he's worth activating.

If you are not yet convinced that a player like Markakis is more valuable than a player like Hollandsworth, let me suggest the following way of thinking about the issue.

Suppose that you have already bought a baseline player to fill the utility spot on your active roster. Now the reserve draft has begun. You can use your first five picks to select five players like Hollandsworth or five players like Markakis. It's extremely unlikely that any of the five Hollandsworths will help you. Even if you have an injury on your active roster, you should be able to pick up someone at least as valuable as Hollandsworth in the free agent pool. But if you have five Markakises, one of the five is very likely to achieve the 400 AB/2.0 SGP scenario by midseason. (Remember, we forecast a 1 in 5 chance that Markakis would become worth activating.) As soon as that happens, you can exercise your call and improve your team.

The upside potential makes the Nick Markakises of the world more valuable than the Todd Hollandsworths. (However, there may be a reason to pick a couple of players like Hollandsworth in the reserve rounds, and I discuss it in Chapter 17.)

Value of Current-Season Put Options

Current-season call options tend to add value to below-baseline players who have some upside potential. Conversely, current-season put options tend to enhance the value of above-baseline players who have some downside potential. Puts tend to be exercised when a player gets injured and suddenly has expected SGPs of zero or when his performance becomes so poor that his expected SGPs fall below the baseline. Otherwise, the analysis for valuing puts is analogous to that for valuing calls.

To illustrate how a put option becomes valuable, suppose you bought into the hype and paid up for Shawn Chacon at the start of the 2006 season. By the end of May, Chacon was struggling with a 5.21 ERA and a 1.68 WHIP, and you were having trouble sleeping on the nights before Chacon's starts. At that point, you had probably dramatically lowered your expectations for Chacon, perhaps assessing his value for the rest of the season at −2.0 SGPs. Fortunately, if you were playing under the Ultra Rules, you could end your suffering by exercising your put option on Chacon.

You would then either have to activate a pitcher from your reserve list or pick up someone from the free agent pool to take his roster spot. As with call options, the value of this alternative active player would determine the exercise price of your put option on Chacon. Assuming you can always tap the free agent pool, the alternative active player will be equivalent to a baseline player. You should always be able to pick up a harmless free agent pitcher, perhaps a middle reliever, whose value is close to the baseline SGP level. Therefore, the exercise price on put options for a given pool of players will be about the same as on call options. In this case, the remaining SGP value of the alternative active pitcher would have been about 0.6 (0.9 * 2/3), making the put option on Chacon worth 2.6 (the difference between 0.6 and −2.0).

Since the exercise price on put options will generally not be much above zero SGPs, the only cases where put options really become valuable are when a player takes on negative SGP value. Hitters can only generate negative SGPs in the batting average category, and even poor hitters drive in a few runs, so their SGP value rarely falls much below zero. Pitchers, however, can produce negative SGPs in two categories — ERA and WHIP — and any pitcher with a high ERA and WHIP is not likely to be winning or saving many games. So it is not uncommon for a struggling pitcher, especially a starting pitcher who is racking up some innings, to have a value of anywhere from −1.0 to −4.0 SGPs. The put options on those pitchers can become very valuable.

While call options are exercised on reserve players or free agents, put options are exercised on active players. In preparing for auction day, therefore, put options are important for players at or above the baseline SGP level. For each such player, we must consider how likely it is that at some point in the season his value will fall below the baseline, and by how much it might fall below. Then, as with calls, we take the average of those values.

The Chacon example described above highlights an important point about the value of options: Their value is based on expected future performance. Exercising your put option on Chacon at the end of May will not erase the poor stats he has produced up to that point. However, if you believe that he will continue to generate negative value in the future, you can prevent any further damage. When player value increases, which often coincides with an increase in playing time (as in the case of Markakis), we can usually spot it very quickly, exercise our call option, and capture almost all of the value. When player value (typically meaning pitcher value) decreases below the baseline level, we usually take a little longer to figure it out, and we suffer some of the negative value before we exercise the put. This makes the value of the put option, though very real, more difficult to estimate than the value of the call.

To consider another very simplified example, suppose we were skeptical about Chacon all along. Going into the season, we thought that there was a 50% chance that he would pitch very well and produce +6.0 SGPs but also a 50% chance that he would flop and produce −3.0 SGPs. We expected the outcome to be clear by the end of May, at which point he would already have realized one-third of his value, positive or negative. Disregarding the put option, we calculated Chacon's expected SGP value as: $(0.5 * 6.0) + (0.5 * -3.0) = 1.5$ SGPs.

However, if the negative scenario comes to pass, we will exercise our put option. We will already have incurred -1.0 SGP in the first one-third of the season, but we will replace Chacon for the second half with a baseline pitcher who provides 0.6 SGPs for the rest of the season. The total value of that pitching slot would then be $-1.0 + 0.6 = -0.4$ SGPs over the entire season. We thus revise our calculation of Chacon's expected SGP value accordingly: $(0.5 * 6.0) + (0.5 * -0.4) = 2.8$ SGPs. The put option on Chacon would be worth 2.6 if we exercise it, and there is a 50% chance we will do so, increasing Chacon's value by 1.3 SGPs $(2.6 * 0.5)$ in the auction.

In practice, calculating precise values for the current-season call and put options is very difficult. I would never suggest that a Roto owner attempt to calculate these values for lots of players before the auction. The time would be better spent in some other aspect of preparation. Having good intuition about option value is quite important, however. As the examples of Nick Markakis and Shawn Chacon should demonstrate, these options can easily change the value of players by as much as one SGP or more, perhaps adding $3 or more to the player's fair auction price. And in the reserve draft, current-season calls are critical in determining the relative value of players.

To help build good intuition about option value, I would suggest attempting to calculate precise option values for a few players who are of particular interest to you, then using them as guides in evaluating other players. In the next chapter, we will discuss how to add these option values to your pricing spreadsheet.

CHAPTER FOURTEEN

Adding Options to Your Pricing Spreadsheet

How you incorporate options into your player prices for the auction will largely depend on how much time you are willing to devote to the process. Many Roto owners may decide, after producing the spreadsheet for Marginal SGP Pricing described in Part I, that they can't stand to do any more number-crunching. Others, who don't make any pretense about having a life, may spend long hours determining option values for large numbers of players.

In this chapter, I will attempt to tread a middle path. I will describe how you can modify your pricing spreadsheet to incorporate options with only a modest investment of time. Saving time will require us to cut some corners, but the resulting analysis will still add significant value to your auction preparation. Even if you do not want to take on this extra work, understanding this method should help you to make "on the fly" adjustments to your Marginal SGP prices to reflect option values. If, on the other hand, you would like to do even more work than detailed here, you'll be able to build upon these methods to generate more complete and precise option values for your players.

Recall that, at the end of Chapter 7, we ended up with the following spreadsheet that had dollar values for all players:

	A	***	R	S	T	U
	Player		SB SGP	TOT SGP	MRG SGP	$$$ VAL
1						
2	Adams		1.2	3.2	2.3	9.3
3	AndersonB		0.5	3.4	2.5	10.1
4	Baldelli		2.1	5.8	4.9	19.0
5	Barajas		0.0	3.5	3.1	12.4
***						
10	Chavez		0.9	6.9	6.0	23.2

The pitchers' spreadsheet had the same three right-hand columns — Total SGPs, Marginal SGPs, and Dollar Value.

To include option values, we will need to start adding columns to the right-hand side of both the hitters' and the pitchers' spreadsheets. For players above the baseline value, we need to consider two types of options, current-season puts and future-season calls. To value these, we will add five columns to each spreadsheet:

	A	* * *	U	V	W	X	Y	Z
1	Player		$$$ VAL	CUR PUT	FUT UP	CALL EX PRC	FUT CALL	RAW OA $$$ VAL
2	**Adams**		9.3					
3	**AndersonB**		10.1					
4	**Baldelli**		19					
5	**Barajas**		12.4					
* * *								
10	**Chavez**		23.2					

The values in the column titled "$$$ VAL" — the dollar values that result from Marginal SGP Pricing — can be considered a player's "initial dollar value" — his value before options are factored in. The other column headings are as follows:

CUR PUT = value of the current-season put option
FUT UP = a player's expected next-year dollar value if he realizes his upside potential
CALL EX PRC = the exercise price of the future-season call option
FUT CALL = the expected value of the future-season call option
RAW OA $$$ VAL = raw option-adjusted dollar value

Rather than proposing complicated formulas for calculating precise option values, I will provide guidelines you can use to make adjustments for those players most likely to have significant option value.

Step 1: Entering Values for Current-Season Put Options

Let's start with current-season puts. If your league rules allow you to reserve a player at almost any time, current-season puts can significantly affect player values. However, if your league restricts your ability to remove a player from your active roster, as the original Roto rules did, then these options will have minimal value; you can leave the CUR PUT column blank and skip to Step 2.

As we discussed in Chapter 13, current-season puts can only have value for players on active rosters. So to begin with, we limit our consideration to the 276 players that have a value above the baseline (that is, an initial dollar value of at least $1). Moreover, put options only have value for players we deem to have a significant risk of producing value well below the level of a baseline player (recall the Shawn Chacon example). Since the baseline SGP levels for different pools of players will typically be no higher than about 1.0 SGP, "well below the baseline" usually means negative SGP value.

The players who carry the highest risk of performing well below the baseline are starting pitchers. The riskiest starters are generally those whose expected values are not much above the baseline in the first place. These are pitchers who will go for under $5 in the auction and will be reserved or released fairly quickly if they turn out to be having a poor season. Although all of them are expected, on average, to be mediocre, some are more reliably mediocre (stable value), while others may either soar or crash and burn (volatile value).

Since we're taking a shortcut approach, we will simply identify the players we deem to have a significant risk of performance well below the baseline and then assign a subjective value of $1, $2, or $3 to each player's put option. The stronger the risk of a sub-baseline performance, the higher the put-option value. You can give the reliably mediocre veterans $1 of current-season put option value. High-risk rookies and rehab projects can get $2 or $3, depending on just how risky you think they are.

Among the group of medium-value starting pitchers — say, those valued between $5 and $12 — the probability of a sub-baseline season will be lower, so put option values should be lower as well. In this echelon, more consistent hurlers get no put-option value, while the more volatile can get $1 or $2 based on your risk assessment. The best starters, those with an initial value of about $12 or higher, should get no put-option value.

Relief pitchers who are good enough to be above the baseline are not likely to produce much negative value; they simply do not pitch enough innings to do much harm in ERA and WHIP. Middle relievers can get $1 of put-option value if you think they are especially risky. Closers should get no put-option value.

Hitters have even less chance than relievers of producing negative SGP value. For almost all hitters, the worst-case scenario is an SGP value of zero, resulting from a season-ending injury, trade to the other major league, or demotion to the minors. Because this risk is usually small, you may not want to assign current-season put value to any of the hitters. At most, you may want to assign a $1 put-option value to a few hitters who have an unusually high chance of turning out to be worthless early in the season. Doug Mientkiewicz and Juan Castro were examples of such hitters in 2006.

As you can see, the number of players to whom you will assign current-season put value is small — probably 40 to 60 players. The total value of these puts will probably be between $50 and $100. Eventually, we will incorporate these puts into new dollar values for players, but for now let's move on to the future-season calls.

Step 2: Estimating Players' Future Potential

Unlike current-season puts, future-season calls apply to a wide number of players. They may add value to any player available in the auction, not just those whose initial dollar values are above the baseline. In fact, once we consider future-season calls, some players who were previously below the baseline level will move into the pool of 276 who should be purchased in the auction. These players, who we feel have limited current-season value but high future potential, will replace other players with slightly more current-season value but little future potential. Therefore, we need to consider the value of future-season calls for all of the players eligible for the auction.

For our shortcut approach, we will make two strong assumptions when assigning future-season call-option values. First, we will only consider the value of the call option for the following season, even though some players will have call options with value two or more years in the future. Call options more than one year in the future are less valuable anyway, since they must be discounted more, so by eliminating them we simplify our task without losing the main benefits of the analysis. However, we will shortchange a few players with high future potential; that's one of the tradeoffs of using a shortcut approach. For these players, you may want to make a generous estimate of the player's next-year option value to offset the neglect of additional future options.

Our second assumption is that the exercise price of the future-season call option is equal to the player's initial dollar value (as derived through Marginal SGP Pricing) or $1, whichever is greater. In reality, the exercise price will be the player's salary, but since the auction hasn't occurred yet we don't know what salaries for the available players will be. We have to make some assumption about exercise price to value the option, and the Marginal SGP Price provides a handy and reasonable estimate of current-season salary for most players above the baseline. For players with the most valuable call options, the initial dollar value may offer an unrealistically low estimate of the player's actual auction price. Later on, we will adjust for this bias. For players below the baseline, we can't assume that they will have a salary of less than $1 (though we may feel their true value is less than $1), so we assume that they will have a salary (and thus a future-call exercise price) of $1.

Every player, if purchased at his initial dollar value, has at least some chance of being a good keeper for next year, so theoretically the future-season call option has at least some value for every player. For most players, though, the potential value of this option is low. We are trying to focus on those individuals where the future-season upside really adds value.

Players with high upside potential usually have two characteristics: 1) they're cheap, and 2) they're young. So to begin with, I suggest skipping over all players with an initial value of $20 or greater and almost all players over 28 years of age. For players with an initial dollar value over $20, the exercise price is so high that the option will almost never add significant value. The likelihood of significant improvement from their current high level of production is limited. And players who are over 28 are unlikely to show dramatic improvement that will raise their auction value substantially for future seasons. Certainly there are exceptions, such as players trying to come back from an injury, and these players should be included in your option analysis. But in general these salary and age guidelines will help you to eliminate quickly the players with the least call-option value so you can focus on those with the greatest.

When considering players in this younger, lower-priced group, ask yourself the question, "What is an optimistic, but reasonable, estimate of this player's value in next year's auction?" What do I mean by "optimistic but reasonable"? Estimate a value that you think the player has only about a 20% chance of meeting or exceeding in next year's auction.

By now, you may be getting familiar enough with dollar values that you can think directly in terms of the player's dollar value for next year. You may look at a promising young second baseman who has an initial dollar value of $6 for this year, and you may intuitively think, "This guy has a 20% chance of being worth $12 in next year's auction." If the dollar values do not yet come to you that readily, you may want to compare the player in question to your forecasts for other players for this year. When you find another player whose expected stats for this year represent an optimistic but reasonable estimate of next year's performance for the player in question, then you can use that second player's dollar value to estimate the first player's next-year dollar value.

Since "optimistic but reasonable next-year dollar value" is a mouthful, I will refer to this as "future upside" ("FUT UP" in the spreadsheet). When you have arrived at an estimate of how much a player should be worth if he realizes his upside potential, enter it in that column of the spreadsheet. We are only going to assign value to the future-season call when a player's FUT UP value is at least $4 greater than his initial dollar value. If the difference is less than $4, then the call option does not have meaningful value in this shortcut approach. (So, for all players who have values less than $4 apart, you can leave the FUT UP column blank or you can input the value, whichever you prefer. If you do input an amount less than $4 above the initial dollar value, though, our spreadsheet formula is going to ignore it anyway.)

By now, a selection from the first few lines of our pitchers' spreadsheet for 2006 might look like this:

	A	* * *	P	Q	R	S	T	U
1	Player		$$$ VAL	CUR PUT	FUT UP	CALL EX PRC	FUT CALL	RAW OA $$$ VAL
2	Affeldt		-7.1					
3	Baker		14	1				
4	Bedard		9.5	1	16			
5	Bonderman		14.7		29			
6	Burgos		2.2		12			
7	CabreraD		9.7	1	15			

Baker, Bedard, and Cabrera had current-season put value going into 2006. All three of these starting pitchers were young and therefore seemed to carry some risk of poor performance.

In considering their potential future values, we recognized that Burgos had the chance to become the closer for the Royals in 2006 and therefore had some obvious FUT UP. We concluded that Bedard, Bonderman, and Cabrera also had some chance for a significant increase in value by the 2007 auction. Bonderman, widely considered to have the potential to become an elite starting pitcher, had the most dramatic upside. Once we have entered FUT UP values for all players who warrant it, we are ready to input the formulas to calculate the future-season call value.

Step 3: Calculating the Expected Value of Future-Season Call Options

To do this, we start with five additional values in the bottom portion of the spreadsheet:

	A	B
270	Minimum Diff	4.0
271	FC Exercise Prob	0.5
272	FC Baseline Value	1.0
273	Discount Factor	0.8
274	Ex Price Adjustmt	0.5

Then we add two formulas to the top portion:

	A	* * *	P	Q	R	S	T	U
1	Player		$$$ VAL	CUR PUT	FUT UP	CALL EX PRC	FUT CALL	RAW OA $$$ VAL
* * *								
5	Bonderman		14.7		29	[f8]	[f9]	

[f8] = if(P5 > 1, P5, 1)
[f9] = if(R5 – S5 < $B$270, 0, $B$274 * $B$273
**   * (($B$271 * (R5 - S5)) - $B$272))**

Note that the formulas are presented for Bonderman, since he has the greatest FUT UP, and therefore reference the fifth row of the spreadsheet. The column titled "CALL EX PRC" contains the exercise price for the future-season call. As we discussed above, we set this value to the player's initial dollar value or $1, whichever is greater.

The formula in the column entitled "FUT CALL" calculates an estimated value for the future-season call option. This formula says, first of all, that if the FUT UP is not at least $4 more than the call exercise price, then we will value the future-season call at zero. If the difference is greater than $4, the formula will calculate an option value as follows:

FUT CALL =
   Exercise price adjustment factor * Discount factor
   *** ((FC Exercise Prob * (FUT UP – CALL EX PRC))**
   – FC Baseline Value).

If you are willing to accept this formula at face value, you can skip the next three paragraphs. If you really want to know the logic behind this equation, here goes:

The difference between the FUT UP and the exercise price equals the value that exercising the call option will have if the player achieves his optimistic but reasonable forecast. We consider this scenario representative of all cases where we decide to exercise the call option for that player. We make a rough estimate of the "exercise probability" of the future-season calls, and we decide that these calls will be exercised about 50% of the time on players with at least a $4 difference between the FUT UP and the exercise price. To get an expected value of the call option at next year's auction, we multiply the exercise probability times the likely value if exercised: 0.5 * (FUT UP – initial dollar value).

We must make three further adjustments, however, before we have an appropriate value for the future-season call for this year's auction. First, we have already acknowledged that all players have at least some future-season call option value. We will make the rough estimate that most players have at least $1 of future-season call value. Therefore, when we calculate the option value for those players with more valuable options, we will subtract $1, so that we are only counting the option value in excess of what the typical player has. In the formula above, this $1 is referred to as the "future-call baseline value." We only give players credit for value above that baseline. For our second adjustment, we must apply our discount factor to the player's future-season call option value, for the reasons we discussed in Chapter 12.

Finally, as alluded to above, our assumption about the exercise price of the future-season calls is, unfortunately, least likely to hold true for just those players who have the most valuable calls. Those players, like Bonderman, are precisely the players who will probably be bid up to a price above their initial dollar value. As their salary goes above their initial dollar value, however, the value of their option, as we have estimated it to this point, will decline. The quantity "FUT UP – initial dollar value" will overestimate the value of the option when the salary is higher than the initial dollar value. There is no way to know before the auction exactly how high the bidding will go on a player, and there is no straightforward way to estimate the value of the call option without knowing the salary level. We deal with this problem by introducing a fudge factor, the "exercise price adjustment factor" in the equation above. This factor, which must be between zero and one, says, in effect, that the salary will almost certainly end up somewhere between the player's initial dollar value and his FUT UP. I am suggesting that you set this value to 0.5, implying that the salary is most likely to end up about halfway in between, and therefore the option will end up having about half as much value relative to our initial assumption about exercise price. During the auction, you should try to keep in mind that, if the bidding on a player stops near his initial dollar value, the call option will be worth a little more, but if the bidding rises to his FUT UP, then the option will be worth less.

The results of these calculations for these six pitchers are:

	A	* * *	P	Q	R	S	T	U
1	Player		$$$ VAL	CUR PUT	FUT UP	CALL EX PRC	FUT CALL	RAW OA $$$ VAL
2	Affeldt		-7.1			1.0	0.0	
3	Baker		14	1		14.0	0.0	
4	Bedard		9.5	1	16	9.5	0.9	
5	Bonderman		14.7		29	14.7	2.5	
6	Burgos		2.2		10	2.2	1.2	
7	CabreraD		9.7	1	15	9.7	0.7	

Affeldt and Baker had no future-season call value, because in their cases their FUT UP was less than $4 above their future call exercise price. The calls for Bedard and Cabrera had a little bit of value, on the chance that they might improve on previous performance in 2006 and significantly boost their auction value for 2007. Burgos had some call value as well, since his value might jump if he were to establish himself as the Royals' closer in 2006 or even in spring training 2007. Bonderman had the most call value because his age, skills, and previous performance indicated there was some chance he could join the pitching elite.

Step 4: Incorporating Option Value into Marginal SGP Pricing

Now that we have estimates for both types of options that apply to players above the baseline, we calculate new "raw option-adjusted dollar values" with the following formula:

	A	***	P	Q	R	S	T	U
1	Player		$$$ VAL	CUR PUT	FUT UP	CALL EX PRC	FUT CALL	RAW OA $$$ VAL
***								
5	Bonderman		14.7		29	14.7	2.5	[f10]

[f10] = P5 + Q5 + T5

The "RAW OA $$$ VAL" is simply the sum of the player's initial dollar value and the value of his two options.

There will be one major problem with these new dollar values, however, which is why I call them "raw": Once we add in option values, the overall value for the top 276 players will add up to substantially more than the $3120 available in the auction. To correct that problem, we need to make one more adjustment. First, we must sort both the hitters' and pitchers' spreadsheets in descending order of "RAW OA $$$ VAL." Then we need to add up the "RAW OA $$$ VAL" values for the top 168 hitters and top 108 pitchers. (You may recall that we followed a similar procedure back in Chapter 7 to convert marginal SGPs to initial dollar values.) Suppose that the total value for these top 276 players is $3500. We enter this total in the bottom of the spreadsheet, along with the total dollars available in the auction:

	A	B
275	Total $$$ in auction	3120
276	Total RAW OA$V	3500

Then we add one more column with one more formula on the right-hand side:

	A	* * *	P	* * *	U	V
1	Player		$$$ VAL		RAW OA $$$ VAL	FIN OA $$$ VAL
* * *						
5	Bonderman		14.7		17.2	[f11]

[f11] = U5 * ($B$275 / $B$276)

This formula scales back the values in the RAW OA $$$ VAL column so that the total for the top 276 players equals the $3120 actually available in the auction. The values in the "FIN OA $$$ VAL" column are the final option-adjusted dollar values that you should use in your auction. These values represent the overall package you get when you buy a player: his expected production for this year, the option to remove him from your roster if his value falls below the baseline, and the option to retain him for future seasons if his value increases above his current salary. These rows of the pitcher spreadsheet would end up looking like this:

	A	* * *	P	* * *	U	V
1	Player		$$$ VAL		RAW OA $$$ VAL	FIN OA $$$ VAL
2	Affeldt		-7.1		-7.1	-6.3
3	Baker		14.0		15.0	13.4
4	Bedard		9.5		11.4	10.2
5	Bonderman		14.7		17.2	15.3
6	Burgos		2.2		3.4	3.0
7	CabreraD		9.7		11.4	10.1

The final option-adjusted dollar values will differ from the initial dollar values in that players with valuable options will have a higher final value, and players whose options are worth little or nothing will have final values that are a bit lower than their initial value. The values go down for the second group because we are dealing with a fixed pool of $3120; if we attribute dollar value to the options, that value has to be taken away from somewhere else. (Values for players with negative raw dollar values, like Affeldt, will actually increase — i.e., become less negative. This result is not strictly accurate, but does not matter since these players should not be purchased in the auction.)

You may notice a few "imperfections" in these final values. The option values will have changed the ranking of players, especially near the bottom of the list. A number of players that were previously above the baseline will have fallen below, and vice versa. This may turn out to be inconsistent with the fact that you were only supposed to assign put-option value to players above the baseline.

Furthermore, the 168th-best hitter and 108th-best pitcher may no longer be worth exactly $1, as they theoretically should be and were in the initial dollar values. That's why I call this the shortcut approach to calculating option values. The goal of this approach is to get the majority of the effect of options built into your prices with an acceptable amount of effort. If you want to apply more effort, you can tinker with the data in your spreadsheet to remove these imperfections, but the additional benefit in the auction will be minimal. The shortcut-derived values, imperfect though they may be, are accurate enough to give you a significant advantage over rival owners — and that's what you're looking for.

* * *

You have now completed the player valuation process for your auction. If your league holds a reserve draft, you can continue to apply option valuation concepts to rank players for the reserve draft as well. You probably should not devote nearly as much time to the reserve draft as to the auction, so I will try to summarize briefly how you might value reserve players. If you want to, you can follow a process similar to the one described above to rank reserve players in a spreadsheet.

For reserve players, two types of options may have value: current-season calls and future-season calls. The first round of the reserve draft is usually devoted to selecting players who were not eligible for the auction but whose options actually make them more valuable than many players purchased late in the auction. As the reserve draft rolls through subsequent rounds, owners should continue to seek the available players with the most option value, be it current-season value or discounted value for future seasons.

A current-season call option has value equal to the expected value of a player's performance above the baseline in the current season. For a player who has no chance of performing above the baseline, either because he will not get to the major leagues or is just not a good player, this call option will have no value. For a player who has some chance of playing well enough that you would want to activate him at some point during the season, you need to estimate the value of that possibility.

Under the official rules, minor leaguers are not eligible for the auction draft. In most seasons there are a few players who are sent down to the minors at the end of spring training but are nearly certain to be called up early in the season and begin contributing to the major league club. These players (Jason Bartlett of the Twins was an example in 2006) may have expected stats that would be worth $5-$10 or more if they were eligible for the auction. These players have the most valuable current-season calls and will be among the first picks in the reserve draft.

Other types of players who have some current-season call value include: players like Nick Markakis, who most likely will not get enough playing time to contribute but will become much more valuable if they do get to play; players, especially starting pitchers, who are not expected to perform well enough to produce value above the baseline but who could become valuable if they raise their performance to a higher level; players on the disabled list who have low-value expected stats for the season, but may increase in value once they return to active play; and minor league prospects who may be called up during the season and begin to contribute. You can make a list of all of the players who may have some value on an active Roto roster during the current season and assign an estimated call option value to each of those players.

In Chapter 13, we estimated current-season call value in terms of SGPs. Here, since we're preparing for the auction and reserve draft (where all other values are expressed in dollars), it will be helpful to convert SGP values into dollar values. In Markakis' case, for instance, we estimated in the last chapter that his current-season call had a 20% chance of being exercised and, if exercised, he would likely produce about 2.0 SGPs. A player with expected stats equivalent to 2.0 SGPs would have an auction value of about $5. (This value is based on the assumptions we have in our spreadsheet from Chapter 7. The baseline value for non-catchers is 0.9 SGPs, and the dollar value of one marginal SGP is $3.69. So an outfielder worth 2.0 SGPs would have a draft value of 1 baseline dollar + [1.1 marginal SGPs * $3.69] = $5.06.) Because Markakis had only a 20% chance of realizing this $5 value, his current-season call for 2006 was worth about $1.

Although the process of expressing current-season calls in terms of dollars may seem cumbersome, it becomes somewhat easier when you have already completed a spreadsheet of player values for the auction. Then, when trying to determine the dollar value that a player might achieve, you can just find another player from the auction who represents the first player's potential upside.

Future-season calls can be valued in much the same way for the reserve draft as for the auction. In fact, the process is a little bit easier because the exercise price of the option is more certain. A player chosen in the reserve draft will typically have a predetermined salary based on his round of selection.

In addition, under the Ultra rules, a player chosen in the reserve draft may qualify to be retained on the reserve roster at an effective salary of zero for the following season, if the player is a major league rookie and has never been active in your Roto league.

To begin to value the future-season call for a reserve player, you should estimate his future upside value the same way you would for an active player. Based on that estimate, you can make an educated guess as to how early or late the player is likely to be picked in the reserve draft. You can then calculate a call value using the same equation as for active players, but without the exercise price adjustment factor:

Reserve player future-season call =
   Discount factor * ((FC exercise prob
   *** (FUT UP – CALL EX PRC))**
   – FC baseline value)

Using the same assumptions for the constant values as we did in our spreadsheet, the equation would become:

Reserve player future-season call =
   0.8 * ((0.5 * (FUT UP – CALL EX PRC)) – $1)

Suppose, for instance, that you are considering a player with a FUT UP of $8 and you do not expect him to qualify to be retained on the reserve roster next spring. If he were picked in a round that would result in a future salary of $8 or more, then his future-season call option would have no value according to this formula. You can therefore make an educated guess that he will be selected in a later round, and his future-season call will have a lower exercise price. You may decide to estimate his future call value based on an exercise price of $5. Based on the formula above, the value of that call would be 0.8 * ((0.5 * ($8 – $5)) – $1) = $0.4.

When drafting, you need to remember the exercise price you assumed and make sure that you do not draft a player in an earlier round, thereby raising the exercise price. If you were to draft him earlier, the future call would not be worth as much as the value you have calculated. On the other hand, if you do not get around to picking this player in a round with a $5 future salary, and he is still available in a round with a $2 future salary, then his future-season call will be worth even more than you calculated. In this example, if the player were not chosen until a round with a $2 future salary, the value of his call for next year would increase to 0.8 * ((0.5 * ($8 - $2)) - $1) = $1.6.

The value of a player in the reserve draft is the sum of the values of his two options — the current-season and future-season calls. These player values do not correspond to an actual dollar amount, as values for the auction do. Instead, they provide a scale for assigning relative values to the players and ranking them in order of desirability.

In theory, once you have your ranked list, you would always want to select the highest remaining player when your turn comes up in the reserve draft. The objective is to acquire the most valuable portfolio of options possible, and your ranked list tells you where the most valuable options remain. As with the auction, this approach would ignore balance on your roster in order to maximize value, under the assumption that you can trade to achieve balance later on.

CHAPTER FIFTEEN
Managing Your Portfolio of Current-Season Options

H opefully, you will emerge from auction day with a valuable portfolio of current-season call options on your reserve roster, as well as some current-season puts on your active roster. These options will only be valuable, though, if you make the right decisions to exercise them throughout the season. Many aspects of the decisions to pick up and drop players were probably clear to you already even if you had never heard the terms "put" and "call," but perhaps some were not. In this chapter, we will discuss how options may affect roster decisions in leagues that allow owners to activate or reserve players at any time.

Call options on your reserve roster during the season

Occasionally, the expected production of one of your reserve players will significantly increase, perhaps as a result of increased playing time, an opportunity to perform in a new role (for example, leadoff hitter or closer), or simply an improvement in performance. An owner needs to assess the value of his reserve players from week to week to determine whether any of them have increased enough in terms of expected production to justify exercising a call option and activating them.

When we considered the value of Nick Markakis' call option, we could project Markakis' production for the entire remainder of the season, since an injury to his competition (David Newhan) and his steady production warranted continued starts in the outfield. Often, however, the assessment of expected production will be based not on the entire remainder of the season but on some shorter period. If a backup third baseman on your reserve roster will be filling in for 2-3 weeks while the regular recovers from a minor injury, then you may want to activate him to take advantage of his increased production in the short term, even though his total value for the season will not have risen very much. The value of the call option would not justify exercising it if you were committed to the player for the rest of the season, but you are not committed. Once the player is active you will have a put option on him, and you will probably exercise that put in three weeks. So you project the value of the backup third baseman and the alternative active player over the next three weeks, and you decide to exercise your call.

As explained in a previous chapter, we assume that the exercise price of any current-season call option equals the value of the baseline player in the league, not the alternative active player on your roster. This is a fair assumption when we are trying to develop a theory that encompasses a variety of circumstances, but in a given situation it may not be a fair assumption. In particular, if your roster is loaded at a particular position, you may find it difficult to clear a spot to activate a reserve player.

One way to clear a spot would be to trade away a player from the logjammed position, but perhaps none of the other owners in your league will give you what you consider a fair trade. Or perhaps you only want to activate a player for a short period, as with the backup third baseman mentioned above. You don't necessarily want to make a major trade just to open up a roster spot for three weeks.

In these situations, you have created an abnormally high exercise price for your call option, making it less valuable. To avoid this problem, I suggest thinking of one hitting slot and one pitching slot on your roster as a "flex slot," where you keep a baseline-type player (unless you have recently exercised a call option).

You do not want to weaken your roster to create a flex slot. But suppose you have a choice between carrying two players worth 3.0 SGPs apiece or, alternatively, one worth 5.0 and another worth 1.0. Both pairs are worth 6.0 SGPs, but if you choose the second pair you can drop the 1.0 SGP player to exercise a call on a reserve player who has suddenly become worth 2.5 SGPs. In effect, the flex slot acts as a check on the exercise price of current-season calls, making it easier for you to realize the value of your options.

Call options in the free agent pool during the season

In addition to the call options you hold on your reserve players, you also potentially hold call options on each player in the free-agent pool. You can buy one of these call options by bidding on a player; if no other owner bids higher on the same player, you own the call option on that player and must immediately exercise it. (You can, however, exercise your put a week later and reserve the player.)

As with the players on your reserve roster, you need to assess the free agents from week to week to determine whether any of them have increased enough in value to justify exercising an option. This task is much more challenging than assessing your reserve roster because so many more players are involved, and you have no particular reason to be following most free agents closely, as you probably do with your reserve players.

Occasionally, you may want to acquire a free agent as soon as you can tell that his call option has value, even if you would not ordinarily want to exercise that option immediately. This situation often arises when a promising rookie is called up to the majors for the first time; although his immediate prospects for playing time may be poor, his current-season or future-season call may be quite valuable. When the Brewers first called up Prince Fielder in 2005, for instance, alert owners recognized not only the value of his expected production over the remainder of 2005 (modest) but also the value of his potential 2006 and 2007 production (significant). Those who bought Fielder's option on the cheap harvested at least one season of excellent performance.

Similarly, if you see a closer starting to struggle, you might want to acquire a free-agent reliever from the same bullpen who might be in line to pick up some saves. In some instances, this tactic will allow you to acquire a player before others are ready to bid on him. If the player does not pan out, you can always reserve or waive him later without much cost.

Put options on your active roster during the season

In many respects, put options on your active players are the flip side of call options on your reserve players. You must monitor the value of your active players from week to week to determine whether any of their expected SGP values for the remainder of the season have fallen below the baseline. In certain circumstances, these occurrences will be obvious. When a player's expected SGP value drops to zero because he is injured, sent down to the minors, or traded to the other major league, you will ordinarily want to exercise your put and remove him from your active roster.

The most difficult exercise decisions arise when a player, especially a pitcher, is still active in the majors but is performing poorly. There is no magic formula for determining whether the player will continue to perform so poorly that he is below the baseline and should be removed from your active roster. You simply have to make your best baseball judgment about whether his woes are temporary or likely to continue. If you reserve the player, you will still have the call option to reactivate him if his performance improves.

When exercising a put, you can either place the player on your reserve roster or waive him. Your course of action should depend on whether you believe the player's current-season or future-season call options have significant value. If you think one or both of those options do have value—that is, you will want the player back on your active roster either later this year or next year—then you ought to reserve the player. If those call options have minimal value, then you may as well waive him.

CHAPTER SIXTEEN
Long-Term Contract Decisions

We can put together all of the pieces we have developed so far to analyze a common decision in Rotisserie with player carryover: the long-term contract decision. When you have a player entering the third year of his contract, you must make one of three choices before auction day. You can 1) cut the player, 2) keep him for one more year at his current salary, after which you must release him, or 3) sign him to a long-term contract for more than one season.

If you sign the player to a long-term deal, his salary will increase by $5 times the number of additional seasons for which he is being signed. If the player's initial salary is $10 and you decide to sign him to a four-year contract (covering the current season plus three more years), his salary would immediately increase to $25 ($10 plus three additional years times $5).

To make the right contract decision, you must know or estimate the following values:

S   the player's current salary
D   the discount factor for your league
V1   the player's expected salary value in the current year
V2   the player's expected salary value in the following year
V3   the player's expected salary value in the year after that
. . . and so on.

In addition, we will create a variable "B" to represent the benefit you get from having that player on your roster.

The benefit of exercising your option to keep the player at his current salary for the current year can be expressed as B = V1 - S. If V1, the player's expected value in the current year, is less than S, his salary, then the benefit of keeping the player is negative, and you simply cut him. You should be able to repurchase the player in the auction, if you want to, at a price below his current salary. If V1 is greater than S, the player is a keeper for the current season.

If you sign the player to a two-year contract, then the benefit you get in the first year declines to V1 – (S + 5), since the player's salary will be $5 greater. At the same time, though, you potentially gain a benefit in the second year of the contract (though it must be discounted, since future value is always worth less than present value). Combining the benefits for each year produces a total benefit for the 2-year contract of

$$B = (V1 - (S + 5)) \; + \; (D * (V2 - (S + 5)))$$

For example, suppose you bought Grady Sizemore for $7 at the start of the 2005 season. He's obviously a keeper going into 2007, but he's in the last year of his contract; if you keep him at $7, you'll have to release him after the season. You believe that Sizemore will be worth $24 in the 2007 auction, and you feel that $24 is also a reasonable estimate of his value in future seasons. (To keep this example simple, we are assuming that V1, V2, and all future values of V equal $24, but many players will have different expected values for future seasons.)

If you decide to keep Sizemore for one more year at his current salary, the benefit to you will be B = $24 – $7 = $17. If you choose to sign him to a two-year contract, his salary will increase to $12. Assuming the discount factor for your league is 0.80, then the total benefit to you will be B = ($24 – $12) + (0.8 * ($24 – $12)) = $12 + $9.60 = $21.60. In the first year, you will receive $12 of benefit (rather than $17) because of Sizemore's salary hike. But you will also expect to get $12 of benefit in 1998, which is discounted to a present value of $9.60.

If you believe that all of the inputs to these equations are correct, then you should prefer signing Sizemore for two years rather than one, because the total benefit of a two-year deal ($21.60) is greater than the benefit of keeping him for one more year ($17). OK, what about a three-year contract? The reasoning is similar, but now the salary increases by $10 rather than $5, and the third-year benefit must be discounted twice. The formula for the total benefit of the three-year contract is:

**B = (V1 – (S + 10))   +   (D * (V2 – (S + 10)))
     +   (D * D * (V3 – (S + 10)))**

For Sizemore, the calculation becomes B = ($24 – $17) + (0.8 * ($24 – $17)) + (0.8 * 0.8 * ($24 – $17)) = $7 + $5.60 + $4.48 = $17.08. The benefit in the first two years is reduced by the higher salary, and, in this case, the reduction outweighs the added value of the third year. The formula and calculation for a four-year contract for Sizemore would be:

**B = (V1 - (S+15)) + (D * (V2 - (S+15))) + (D*D* (V3 - (S+15)))
     + (D*D*D* (V4 - (S+15))).**

**B = ($24 - $22) + (0.8 * ($24 - $22)) + (0.8 *0.8 * ($24 - $22))
     + (0.8 * 0.8 * 0.8 * ($24 - $22))
     = $2 + $1.60 + $1.28 + $1.02
     = $5.90.**

Table 16-1 summarizes our analysis of the long-term contract decision for Sizemore. In this example, the two-year contract is the best choice. You can apply these formulas to any player in the last year of his contract to calculate which contract length will produce the maximum future benefit.

Table 16-1

Length of contract	Expected benefit
1 year	$17
2 years	$21.60
3 years	$17.08
4 years	$5.90

Based on these formulas, we can make a few general statements about long-term contracts. First, the higher the discount factor for your league, the less beneficial long-term contracts will be, because the benefit you get in future seasons will be worth less in the present. However, even if we assume a discount factor of 1.0, a long-term contract doesn't make sense unless V2, the player's expected salary value in the following year, is at least $10 greater than his current salary. If V2 is only $10 greater than S, then the benefit of the second year of the contract, which increases the player's salary by $5, will be the discounted value of $5. This will not outweigh the $5 of benefit that you lose in the first year due to the salary increase.

Following similar reasoning, if V3 is not at least $20 greater than S, then there is no way that a three-year contract can be more beneficial than a two-year contract. And if V4 is not at least $30 greater than S, then you can skip the calculation for the four-year contract.

In general, you may occasionally find two-year contracts to be beneficial, but you will rarely find three-year contracts to be, and I have a hard time even imagining a scenario where a four-year contract is worthwhile.

A couple of other considerations may affect decisions on long-term contracts. First, the official Roto rules state that a long-term contract is not binding if the player is in the other major league on auction day (e.g., if you are in an AL Roto league, and the player is traded to the NL). In that event, the player is simply released from your roster with no penalty. That possibility is not captured in the above equations. If you want to reflect it, you can multiply the discount factor for each season by your estimate of the probability that the player will remain in the same league before that season.

If, for instance, your league's discount factor is 0.8 and you believe that there is a 90% chance that the player will stay in his current league for the second year of his contract, then you can use a modified discount factor of 0.8 * 0.9 = 0.72. Incorporating this possibility into the equations will reduce the benefit of long-term contracts, as it should. Why pay the player a higher salary this year if he may be out of the league next year, leaving you without the second-year benefit?

The second consideration is that, if an owner does not wish to retain a player in the second or subsequent year of a long-term contract, he or she can buy out the contract for a fee and release the player. Arguably, because of this rule, we should value each future year of the contract as a call option. After all, if by the second year of the contract the player's expected value has fallen below his salary, then the owner can release him.

I prefer to disregard this factor in valuing long-term contracts, for two reasons. First, long-term contracts involve high-value players at relatively low salaries, so the probability that a player's value will fall below the salary of his contract is fairly low. Second, the buy-out fee for a long-term contract is stiff, at least $100. Consequently, most owners are reluctant to buy out these contracts unless the player's value is well below the salary, and, if they do so, they incur a significant cost. Therefore, it is reasonable, as well as simpler, to forget about the buyout option when analyzing a long-term contract.

CHAPTER SEVENTEEN

Tying Up Loose Ends

I have used Option-Adjusted Marginal SGP Pricing myself for a number of seasons, and I believe that it comes very close to providing optimal values for auction day, as well as an optimal basis for making decisions about transactions during the rest of the year. Yet the complexities and subtleties of Rotisserie baseball, not to mention major league baseball, make it virtually impossible to address every issue that might affect player valuation. In this chapter, I will discuss a few issues that we have not yet addressed and how they might — or might not — affect the player values generated using Option-Adjusted Marginal SGP Pricing.

Spending your entire budget

When you go into an auction with dollar values for each player, one of your main objectives is to buy players for less than the value you believe they are worth. This cannot be your sole objective, though. If you spend $5 to buy a player worth $10, that would be a nice purchase. But if you do that 23 times, you will have spent only $115 and filled your roster with only $230 worth of talent. Another owner who has simply paid fair value for his 23 players but has spent his entire $260 budget would end up with a better team than you.

The overriding objective is to fill your roster with as much value as possible. This requires meeting two subordinate objectives: 1) buying players for less than you believe they are worth, and 2) spending your entire budget. Because of the importance of this second objective, very good players rarely seem to be available for less than their fair value. Owners realize that they have to spend their money somewhere, and they seize the opportunity to spend a big chunk of it when they know they are getting value for their money. They figure that they can find their bargains among the medium- and lower-value players.

I believe that this behavior is rational. You should be willing to buy one, two, or even three top players for fair value or very close to it and look to buy under fair value for the rest of your roster. Otherwise, you are likely to fill your entire roster with medium- and low-priced players and find yourself with money left over at the end of the auction.

Does this suggest that we should modify our dollar values to make the top players worth a bit more and the bottom players worth a bit less? Perhaps, but trying to do so might create a problem worse than the one it solves. The new problem would arise because, once you have bought your two or three high-priced players, you would no longer need these adjustments. Once you have spent, say, $65 on two star players, you have only $195 left to spend on 21 more roster spots. At that point, you are unlikely to have much difficulty spending the rest of your budget, so there is no longer any reason to overvalue the top players and undervalue the bottom players. Unfortunately, if you have made these adjustments, your values would be steering you away from the cheaper players that you could afford and toward the pricey players you could not.

Therefore, until someone can convince me that there is a better way to deal with this issue, I think it makes more sense to stick with Marginal SGP Pricing as outlined, without trying to make any further adjustments. In using Marginal SGP Pricing, though, be cognizant of the need to spend your entire budget, and be willing to pay fair value for a couple of top players.

Talent that becomes available after auction day

In Peter Golenbock's *How to Win at Rotisserie Baseball* (1996 edition), Les Leopold wrote a chapter describing his methodology for determining player dollar values. In it, he raises a point that offers a serious challenge to Marginal SGP Pricing. Leopold observes that more value becomes available after the auction in certain categories than in others. The results of actual Roto leagues reveal that much more additional value becomes available during the season in three of the pitching categories — wins, ERA, and WHIP — than in the other five categories. This additional value comes from players who either were not on a major-league roster at auction time or were not considered good enough to be bought in the auction. Leopold therefore concludes that we should pay less for production in these three categories at the auction because, relative to the other five, we can pick up more of it as the season progresses.

I believe that Marginal SGP Pricing, by virtue of its construction, produces values that are not substantially altered by this consideration. First, the values for SGP denominators are based on actual season-end results, so they reflect the value contributed by players acquired in midseason (and the fact that this value will have more effect on some categories than on others). Second, more value becomes available in wins, ERA, and WHIP because, presumably, starting pitchers tend to be less consistent and more subject to injury than other players. However, in Marginal SGP Pricing, player values are based on expected stats. If we have estimated our expected stats correctly, they will reflect starting pitchers' propensities for injuries and bad years, and so will our SGPs.

In short, our SGP values for starting pitchers, as well as for middle relievers, should accurately reflect the expected number of points that these players will gain for us in the year-end standings, just as our SGP values do for all other players. Furthermore, the wins, ERA, and WHIP that do become available during the season tend to come in small packages. It is not as if a team can purchase a bunch of $1 starting pitchers in the auction and expect to finish first — or even close to first — in these pitching categories by tapping its reserve list and the free agent pool.

Therefore, I am not convinced that we should pay any less for marginal SGPs in these three categories than for marginal SGPs in the other five. And yet, I admit, I am not totally convinced that we should pay as much, either. Perhaps Leopold is on to something, and perhaps the greater supply of wins, ERA, and WHIP available during the season somehow makes these marginal SGPs worth less in the auction.

Position flexibility

Some players enter the auction eligible at more than one position, and some others, though not eligible at extra positions on auction day, are likely to become so early in the season. Having players with position flexibility gives you more flexibility in managing your roster during the season, sometimes yielding significant benefits when you have to make player moves. Should you therefore be willing to pay more for these players?

I agree that this flexibility is a beneficial characteristic for a player, but I do not know of any way to quantify it. In general, I do not think it is worth enough that we should factor it into our dollar values for the auction. If the dollar values of two players were equal, though, I would favor a player with multiple position eligibility, especially for low-value players near the end of auction.

The value of position flexibility diminishes as a team has more of it. If you have one outfielder who can also play first base, that can be helpful. If you already have two such outfielders, adding a third is not likely to help much.

Punting one or two categories

Some Roto analysts have devoted much discussion to strategies that involve throwing in the towel on one or two categories and devoting all of your dollars in the auction to the remaining six or seven categories. The thinking behind this approach is that, while you know you will earn only one standings point in any category that you punt on, your increased resources in the other six or seven should give you a large advantage in those. If you can place at or near the top in all of the other categories, you can still win your league, or at least finish in the money.

If you want to, you can easily adjust your spreadsheet to implement a punting strategy. Simply raise the SGP denominator to a very high value, perhaps 1000 times its normal value, in any category you want to punt on. As a result, players will get virtually no credit for SGPs in that category and their dollar values will only reflect their expected production in the categories where you are trying to compete. Remember to sort the players by their new marginal SGPs and enter the new value for total marginal SGPs available in the appropriate cell in the spreadsheet.

Selecting "placeholder" players in the reserve draft

In Chapter 13, I tried to convince you to avoid players like Todd Hollandsworth who have expected value below the baseline and none of the upside potential that would give their call options value. Actually, though, having one or two hitters and pitchers of that sort on your reserve roster can be helpful, albeit indirectly. The reason is this...

In many leagues, in order to purchase a player from the free agent pool, you must simultaneously waive a player from your active roster. When a top player on your team is put on the disabled list for a few weeks, you may want to acquire a free agent, but you certainly do not want to waive the valuable player you are replacing temporarily. Nor do you want to waive a player having high-value options. Instead, you would prefer to reserve the injured player, activate a low-value player like Todd Hollandsworth from your reserve list, and waive the latter when you purchase the free agent. To be eligible for promotion from your reserve to your active roster, a player must be on the active roster of his major league team. Having a couple of reserve players like Hollandsworth, who despite being worth little are almost sure to be active in the majors throughout the season, can make the free-agent bidding process painless when the time comes.

"Friction" in the trading market

I have stated many times in this book that you should focus exclusively on acquiring maximum value on auction day and that if this approach results in imbalances on your roster, you can trade to correct those imbalances later. For instance, if you are strong in certain categories and weak in others, you can trade away players from your stronger categories to shore up the weak areas. Or if you have stocked your reserve roster with players expected to be valuable next year but you need a replacement at shortstop right now, you can trade one of your valuable prospects to get that shortstop. As long as you are able to make fair-value exchanges in the trades, your initial advantage in overall value should carry your team to victory.

In practice, however, making those fair-value trades is not so easy. When markets do not operate as smoothly in practice as they should in theory, economists say there are "frictions" in those markets.

There may be several sources of friction in the trading market in your Roto league. To begin with, there are only 11 other owners with whom you can trade. Some of these owners may not like to trade, or they may be very difficult to deal with. Those may happen to be the owners who have the types of players you need in a trade. Even if you find an owner who is willing or eager to trade, the two of you may have a hard time agreeing on what constitutes a fair-value exchange. After all, an owner usually owns a player because he thought the player was worth more than anyone else did, so getting that owner to exchange the player for what you think is fair value may be tough.

If there's a lot of friction in your league, you may need to pay more attention to balancing your roster in the auction, at the expense of maximizing value. Before the auction, you should consider whether you will be able to trade easily in your league or whether you will have to give up a lot of value to get trades done. If you are concerned about your chances of making fair trades during the season, you may have to be more aggressive in trying to assemble a balanced roster at auction time.

* * *

I do not pretend to have the ultimate answer to Roto performance valuation. At least, not yet. I do hope that this book has provided you with plenty of new ideas on the subject and that those ideas will help you have a more successful auction and season. I also hope that this book rekindles discussion about the topic of performance valuation in general. Thanks for reading.

Chicago, IL
January 2007

PART THREE
Essays

The following essays originally appeared on the BaseballHQ.com web site. They have been revised for publication in this book.

The Impact of Draft Inflation on Pre-Draft Transactions

In Rotisserie leagues that allow owners to carry players over from one season to the next, inflation plays a critical role in auction drafts. Owners naturally choose to retain those players whose salaries are lower than their fair value in the auction. Therefore, owners are left with "too many" dollars to spend in the auction for the players that are available. The result, often termed "'draft inflation," is that players available in the auction cost more than they would in a league that was drafting entire rosters from scratch.

While the impact of inflation on draft pricing has been much discussed in the Roto literature, less attention has been paid to the effect of draft inflation on transactions leading up to the draft. If your Rotisserie league allows you to carry players over from last season, you have two types of transactions you need to consider before your draft: 1) off-season trades and 2) the roster freeze, in which you must decide which players from your winter roster to retain going into the draft. The level of expected inflation in your draft should impact your decisions on both types of transactions.

When making off-season trades, you should think about player values in terms of their inflation-adjusted values, reflecting what they would cost in your league's draft, not in terms of published, non-inflated values. If you are evaluating a trade with similar amounts of value on each side, this distinction may not be significant. However, many off-season trades involve vastly different amounts of value, as trades may be driven by the perceived cheapness of the players involved, rather than their overall value.

To illustrate, suppose you participate in a standard NL Roto league and you are anticipating 25% inflation in your upcoming 2006 draft. On your winter roster, you have Albert Pujols at $47, $1 less than the pre-inflation value you are projecting for him. Another owner offers you a $2 Xavier Nady for Pujols. Nady is clearly a bargain at $2, as you project him to be worth $9.

Should you make the trade? (In order to focus on the inflation issue, let's set aside for a moment any other considerations about the merits of this trade – and there are several.) In a draft with no inflation, this looks like a good trade. Instead of freezing Pujols at $47, you would freeze Nady at $2 and have an additional $45 to spend in the draft. If you simply acquire $45 of value with that money, in addition to the $9 value of Nady, you end up with $54 in value rather than the $48 of value you would have had in Pujols.

Going into a draft with 25% inflation, though, this trade becomes disadvantageous. Pujols' inflation-adjusted value increases to $59.75, while Nady's rises to $11. (Technically, inflation does not affect the first dollar of a player's value, but affects the portion of his value above the first dollar.) The additional $45 to spend in the draft will not allow you to make up the gap between the two.

By using inflation-adjusted values to assess the trade, you account for the fact that any imbalance in salaries will have to be spent in the inflated draft environment. Note that the only salaries that matter in this respect are those of the players whom you would freeze. If you are throwing a player into a deal whom you did not intend to retain, then that player's salary need not enter the calculations.

Just as you should use inflation-adjusted values in evaluating trades, you should also do so in making roster freeze decisions. If Albert Pujols is worth $48 on Draft Day, he will surely cost more in a league with 25% inflation. So while freezing Pujols at $50 might not make sense in a league with no inflation, it would be the right move in a league with high inflation.

On the other hand, even though Pujols might have an inflation-adjusted fair value of $59.75 in a league with 25% inflation, you should not necessarily freeze him with a $58 salary. In any league, with or without inflation, the decision to freeze a player is equivalent to a decision to purchase the player at his prior salary. In weighing whether to freeze Pujols at $58, you should consider all of the same factors that you would consider in whether to pay $58 for him in the draft, given the information that is available to you at the time of roster freeze. But you should be aware of how inflation is likely to affect his value in the draft.

But wait, you might object, how can I incorporate the effect of inflation into off-season trades and roster freeze decisions when the amount of inflation is not determined until after all owners have made their roster freeze decisions? In fact, the exact level of inflation will continue to change right up until Draft Day as player values continue to change.

You cannot make an exact calculation, but you should be able to make a fairly accurate estimate. The level of inflation is largely determined by those players whose values are significantly greater than their salaries, i.e., by the players who are obvious keepers. Players who are marginal keepers will have only a slight effect on inflation, so you don't really need to know which of those players your rival owners will be retaining.

By reviewing the rosters in your league, identifying the obvious keepers, and making reasonable guesses about the rest, you can make a preliminary estimate of draft inflation and use it as described above to aid in your pre-draft decisions.

SGP Denominators for Non-Standard Categories

If your Rotisserie league uses one or more non-standard categories, you have both a problem and an opportunity. Your problem is that most published player values are based on either the original eight Roto categories or on the "5x5" format, which typically adds runs scored for hitters and strikeouts for pitchers. These published values simply will not be accurate for your league's draft.

All of the other owners in your league face the same problem, however, and that creates your opportunity. If you can appropriately value player performance in your non-standard categories, then you will have a significant edge over your competitors. This essay aims to help you do just that, building on my methods for standard categories.

In any category, standard or non-standard, the measure of player value in Roto is the same: how much will a player's performance in that category help a team in the standings of a typical Roto league? Suppose, for example, that 9.5 HRs and 3.4 wins can both be expected to gain a team one point in the league standings. Then we can use the following formulas to compute standings gain points (SGPs) for HRs or wins:

HR SGP = HR / 9.5
Wins SGP = Wins / 3.4

By analyzing the results of the many leagues that use standard categories, we can get a very good idea of what kind of performance it takes to produce one SGP in those categories. On the other hand, because use of the non-standard categories is limited, determining accurate formulas for SGPs becomes more difficult. Based on the data I have been able to review, here are the formulas for seven of the more popular non-standard categories:

Slugging percentage
Slg SGP =
$$(((2453 + (Slg * AB)) / (5500+AB)) - 0.446) / 0.0055$$

On-base average

OBA SGP =

$$(((2135 + \text{Hits} + \text{BB}) / (6100 + \text{AB} + \text{BB})) - 0.350) / 0.0027$$

(The OBA formula is simplified to exclude HBP and SF, which are technically part of the calculation.)

Net steals

SB-CS SGP = (SB - CS) / 5.5

Total bases

TB SGP = TB / 98.0

Hits

H SGP = H / 52.0

Runs produced

RP SGP = RP / 42.0

Net wins

W-L SGP = (W - L) / 2.25

Because of the relatively limited data available, I have not attempted to differentiate between AL and NL Roto leagues. You can use these formulas for either league. Although they might not be quite as accurate as the formulas for the standard categories, they will probably give you something far more reliable than your competitors are using.

If your league uses a non-standard category other than these, you can apply the same principles to develop your own SGP formula. You will have to make your own best estimate of the performance required to produce one SGP.

If your league has used the same category in previous seasons, you can look at the standings from those seasons to get a sense of the differences separating teams in that category. You can use the standings of other leagues too, if you know of any.

As a last resort, you can simply take your best guess at an SGP denominator based on your familiarity with how individual players tend to perform in that category. As long as your estimated SGP denominator is better than whatever method your rivals are using, you should have an advantage.

Future-Season Value Case Study

How much are you willing to pay for Henry Thumper in your draft this spring? Thumper recently learned that a torn biceps tendon will keep him sidelined for the entire upcoming season. He seems to have a solid chance, though, to return to his typical 30+ HR form next year.

If you play in a league that drafts entire rosters from scratch each year, then you would not want to spend even $1 on Thumper. If your league allows you to carry over players from season to season, however, the question of how much to pay for Thumper becomes important. As a player who has no value this season, but may well be worth over $20 in next year's draft, Thumper provides an interesting case study in how to value players whose worth might increase significantly in future seasons.

By purchasing such a player in this year's draft, you give yourself an option to retain that player next year at this year's salary. If, going into next year's draft, the player appears to be worth less than this year's salary, then this option has no value. Your correct move is to release the player back into the free agent pool before the draft, which should make him available at a lower price.

If, on the other hand, the player is worth more than this year's salary in next year's draft, you should exercise your option and retain him on your roster. If his draft value barely exceeds his salary, then your option is only worth a little, but if his draft value greatly exceeds his salary, then your option is worth a lot. Therefore, the value of the option at this year's draft depends on both the probability that it will be exercised next year and the range of values it will have if exercised.

Because of the difficulty in performing a precise calculation of this option value, I've developed a shortcut method for estimating future-season option value. To apply this shortcut method for a particular player, you begin by coming up with an optimistic but reasonable assessment of that player's value in next year's draft. If you would like a more exact definition of "optimistic but reasonable," consider it to be the value that the player has a 20% chance of meeting or exceeding in next year's draft.

Let's take Thumper as an example. The pessimistic scenario is that he struggles to come back from his injury next spring, depressing his draft value substantially below his typical past levels. The middle-of-the-road outlook would be that Thumper reports to spring training healthy next year, but looks a little rusty, and Roto owners cautiously value him somewhat below his historical levels.

Optimistically, though, he may have a smooth rehabilitation, return to spring training in excellent shape, put up big spring numbers, and command a value in line with his performances in pre-injury seasons. After thinking this over, you conclude that Thumper has a 20% chance of being worth $22 or more in next year's draft, so $22 is your optimistic but reasonable future value for him.

As a rule of thumb, in this year's draft, you should be willing to pay no more 25% of the difference between a player's value this year and your optimistic but reasonable assessment of his value for next year. In Thumper's case, then, since we are assuming his value for this year is $0, you should be willing to pay no more than about $5 (25% x $22 = $5.5) this spring. If you can purchase Thumper for less than that, you are getting a bargain.

Several factors contribute to this 25% rule of thumb. First, remember that we're basing this calculation on an optimistic scenario, which has only a modest chance of actually occurring. Second, the value derived from exercising this option, if any, will not accrue until next year, and we always must discount value in the future.

Perhaps most importantly, each dollar spent above a player's current-season value is not only a dollar for which you will see no return this year, but, by increasing the player's salary for next year, it also reduces the value of your future-season option. As such, be cautious about overpaying for a player whose primary value lies in the future. In effect, for every $1 that you overpay, you are wasting $2.

However, since many owners do not understand future-season options or prefer to focus on this year, players with high future value may offer the biggest bargains of your draft.

Drafting to Optimize Option Value

When you walk out of your Rotisserie League draft, the most important question to ask yourself is "How much player value do I have on my roster?"

The second-most important question may be "How much option value do I have on my roster?"

"Option value" refers to the value you gain by assembling a roster with flexibility and upside potential. A roster with high option value offers greater opportunities to respond to setbacks and to seize chances to improve as the season progresses. If you can put together a roster with high option value, the benefits you accrue over the course of the season can be comparable to spending ten to twenty-five extra dollars in the draft. In this essay, we will consider a few ways to capture high option value.

1. Favor players who qualify at multiple positions. Like major league general managers, most Roto owners recognize the benefit of having players who can play at multiple positions. Carrying a couple of these players can make just about any in-season transaction easier. Whether you want to trade, replace an injured player, or bid on a free agent, the ability to shift players on your active roster to new positions can sometimes determine whether you can make the transaction or not.

While the ability to play both corner infield positions or both middle infield positions can be helpful, the most valuable form of position versatility in Rotisserie is when a player qualifies at more than one of the four position player groupings: catcher, corner infielder, middle infielder, or outfielder. Consider bidding an extra dollar on such versatile players.

Another less obvious way to create versatility is to draft players who don't qualify at multiple positions on draft day, but are likely to early in the new season. In a typical spring, a handful of players enter the season expected to play regularly at a position for which they do not already qualify. Even if a player appears at a new position only a platoon basis, he will qualify there for Roto purposes before the end of April.

2. Create "flex slots" on your active roster. Many Roto experts recommend avoiding the top-priced stars in the draft and spreading your money around to diversify your risk. I agree with this reasoning to some extent, but it's definitely possible to carry this idea too far.

When you reach the late stages of the draft, you create a more flexible roster if you park most of your remaining money in fewer players, and spend only $1 or $2 on your last couple of hitters and pitchers. Think of these $1 or $2 players as "flex slots" on your roster that you can use if you want to activate a reserved player, bid on a free agent, or make an unbalanced trade.

Because these last few players cost so little, you probably won't be giving up much when you make moves to replace them. If you were to take your last $30 and spread it evenly among your last six players, you wouldn't be able to take advantage of an opportunity to add a player to your roster without removing a $5 player. You'll have more option value on your roster if you can spend $24 on two players (without overpaying for them, of course) and fill out your last four slots with $1 and $2 guys.

3. Purchase risky players at the end of the auction. On the other hand, just because you're only spending $1 or $2 on these last few players doesn't mean you want to waste it. At least, give yourself a chance to get a bang for your buck. Why bother with someone who might earn $2, but almost surely won't have a chance to do much more?

Instead, gamble on some players who might be a bust, but also have significant upside if they get the right opportunity. If these players in your flex slots do turn out to be busts, you can easily replace them. If they all pleasantly surprise, and you effectively end up without any flex slots, you have a nice problem. You can always try to make a two-for-one or three-for-two trade if you need to create an open slot.

4. Pick the reserve players with the highest upside. Likewise, when you select your reserve roster, focus on players with strong upside potential. You don't help yourself much by stockpiling mediocre middle relievers or no-hit glove men. If you're just looking for a warm body, there are always a few in the free agent pool.

Players with high upside who are likely to be available in the reserve rounds include risky starting pitchers, long-shot closer candidates, and top minor leaguers who may be called up during the season.

By combining each of these tactics as the circumstances of your draft allow, you can build substantial option value into your roster. You will enjoy the benefits gradually over the course of the season, as you repeatedly outmaneuver your opponents and exploit opportunities to improve your team.

Revising Player Values
During the Season

Rotisserie owners usually think about player valuation in conjunction with their draft, but knowing just how much a player is worth can be important during the season as well, particularly when you are evaluating trade possibilities.

The basic measure of a player's value is the same whether you're preparing for Draft Day or considering a late-season deal. What you need to know is: How many points will this player gain for me in my league's standings? Obviously, you want to make trades when you can acquire more points in the standings than you are giving away.

Just as in preparing for the draft, the first step in valuing a player during the season is to come up with the best estimate of his expected stats for the remainder of the season. You can project these stats yourself or consult a web site that offers such projections. In either case, make sure that the projected stats you use reflect the latest available information about the player's likely performance through September.

Once you have your best projection of the player's performance for the rest of the season, you need to convert those stats into standings gain points (SGPs), the number of points that those stats will likely be worth in your league standings. Using the formulas from Chapter 3 of this book will give you player SGP values for a typical team in a typical league. If these were the correct formulas for all Roto owners to use, then the only time that owners should make trades would be when they disagree about the expected performance of one or more players.

Of course, many trades do take place for just that reason. But trades often take place for another reason: depending on the situations of particular teams in a particular league, the same set of stats may have different SGP values.

Before the season, the formulas discussed in Chapter 3 are appropriate for just about any team, because an owner can hardly predict whether or not he will be in a tight race in a given category. As the season progresses, however, and the standings start to sort themselves out, the SGP value of a specific stat will change depending on a team's situation.

Then, to determine appropriate player values you must adjust the SGP formulas according to your specific situation. Here are a few common scenarios with the corresponding adjustment to the formula:

Tight categories. If your team is in a tight race in a particular category, then any contribution in that category is more likely to help your team in the standings. To reflect this, you should lower the denominator in the formula for that category. For instance, my AL formula for home runs is:

HR SGP = HR / 9.5

The value 9.5 represents the average difference between teams in the HR category at the end of the season. If teams are bunched together in HRs in your league, you may want to lower this value to, say, 6.0. Then, a player expected to hit 19 more HRs will be worth a bit more than three standings points to you, rather than just two.

Spread-out categories. As you might expect, you can reverse the logic above if a category is unusually spread out. If that were the case in HRs, you might want to increase the denominator in the formula to 14, which would make you more likely to trade away a power hitter.

First place/last place. If your team is comfortably in first place in a particular category, then you can forget about the formula when considering whether to acquire a certain player. There's nothing that player can do to help you in that category — his SGPs are zero. Likewise, if you're in last, you need not calculate the value you will lose in that category by trading away a certain player. You have no more points to lose.

Rate categories. In counting categories, like HRs, a given performance will help most teams in your league by about the same amount. But in rate categories, like BA, ERA, and WHIP, player stats that will help one team might hurt another. A player expected to bat .270, for example, might lower the BA of the top teams in that category, but he would raise the BA of the bottom teams.

To adjust the SGP formula for your own analysis,

substitute your team's expected BA for the league average BA provided in the formula. Specifically, if your team is on track for a .265 average, instead of using the standard formula:

BA SGP =
(((1472 + Hits) / (5450 + AB)) - 0.2701) / 0.00182,

you should use:

BA SGP =
(((1444.3 + Hits) / (5450 + AB)) - 0.265) / 0.00182.

Make sure you adjust the number of hits at the beginning of the formula to be consistent with the BA you plug in near the end. In this case:

0.265 BA x 5450 AB = 1444.3 hits.

A given player's performance in a rate category can also affect teams differently because different teams will accumulate different totals of at-bats or innings pitched. In BA, for example, the impact of a particular player will be higher if the team's at-bats are lower, and vice versa.

The value of 5450 in the BA SGP equation above is intended to represent 13/14 of the number of at-bats the average team accumulates – that is, the number of at-bats a team will have before it adds its last hitter. If your team is on track for a significantly higher or lower number of at-bats, you may want to adjust this value accordingly in the equation. Just remember to adjust the value for hits accordingly too.

One thing you should notice right away about these calculations is that a player will help you more in the standings if you acquire him earlier in the season. A slugger will move your team up more places in the HR category if you trade for him in May than if you wait until August to acquire him.

So, there's no time like the present to start evaluating trade possibilities.

Making the Most of Your Transaction Dollars

In many Rotisserie leagues, owners spend more on transactions during the season than they do on the draft. And yet, in spite of all the published advice about how to spend your money on Draft Day, very little has been written about how to make the most of your transaction dollars.

Of course, some Roto owners choose to ignore the economic implications of their transactions. Especially in leagues that play for relatively small dollar amounts, owners may choose to take a "win at all costs" approach and spend on any transaction that improves their team the slightest bit.

That is an owner's right, but if you would like an analytical framework to determine whether any potential transaction is worth the cost, this essay will provide such a method. The examples in this essay are based on the official rules for a Rotisserie Ultra league, but you should be able to adapt these concepts to the specific rules of your own league.

If you are trying to optimize your transaction spending, you should only make moves that you expect to increase your year-end prize money payoff by more than the cost of the transaction. In other words, you should not make a transaction that costs $10 unless you believe that the transaction increases the amount of money you can expect to win at the end of the season by more than $10. To evaluate the impact of a transaction on expected prize payoff, we first need to quantify how player performance relates to position in the final standings and, therefore, to prize money.

My analysis of standard 12-team Rotisserie leagues with eight categories shows that the typical difference between teams in the year-end standings is about 4.4 points. Suppose the average team in a hypothetical league spends $500, making the total prize pool worth $6000. Using the 50%-20%-15%-10%-5% payoff schedule in the official rules, the final standings and prize payoffs in this hypothetical average league will look like this:

Place	Points	Prize Money
1st	76.2	$3000
2nd	71.8	1200
3rd	67.4	900
4th	63.0	600
5th	58.6	300
6th	54.2	0
7th	49.8	0
8th	45.4	0
9th	41.0	0
10th	36.6	0
11th	32.2	0
12th	27.8	0

To determine the expected dollar value of one point in the standings, we can run a regression on this data. Based on this hypothetical league, the regression calculation indicates that a gain of one point in the standings (one standings gain point, or SGP) is worth about $43. If we expected the standings to be tighter or the pool to contain more money, then the value of one SGP would increase. If the opposite were true, then the value of one SGP would decrease.

(A regression is a statistical calculation that estimates the relationship between two variables, in this case, standings points and prize dollars. To recreate the regression calculation above using Microsoft Excel, you can enter the standings points in cells B1 through B12 of a spreadsheet, then enter the prize payoffs in cells C1 through C12. Finally, in another cell in the spreadsheet, enter the formula "=SLOPE (C1:C12,B1:B12)". This formula should produce a value of 42.91.)

Assuming that each SGP is worth $43, we can compare the cost of a potential transaction to the number of SGPs we expect to add by making the transaction. If the value of the additional SGPs exceeds the cost of the transaction, then the transaction is worthwhile.

Let's consider a couple of examples from the 2006 NL season. Suppose you have Todd Helton on your active roster, and Helton was just placed on the 15-day DL because of an illness. You need to decide whether to reserve Helton and activate the best alternative hitter on your reserve list, Olmedo Saenz, while Helton is out. Helton does not appear likely to miss much more than the minimum 15 days.

You anticipate that, while Helton is disabled, Saenz might produce one HR, four RBI, no SBs, and a .280 BA in about 25 ABs. Based on the NL SGP formulas in Chapter 3, these statistics would translate into about 0.27 SGPs. Since these additional SGPs are only worth about $12 (0.27 * $43 = $11.61) and the total cost of reserving Helton and activating Saenz is $20, this transaction does not appear to be cost-effective.

In fact, this kind of analysis will usually show that replacing players with short-term injuries is not worthwhile, especially when you consider that you will probably want to spend another $20 to reverse the original transaction when the injured player becomes available again.

Another typical transaction decision arises when a player on your reserve list suddenly increases in value and you must decide whether to activate him. Suppose your reserve list includes Takashi Saito, who appears to have emerged as the Dodgers' closer. You are wondering whether to activate Saito and reserve a marginal middle reliever on your active roster.

In this case, you would expect to gain Saito's stats for the remainder of the season, while giving up the middle reliever's. You project that Saito will collect three wins and 20 saves over the rest of the season, which, combined with a below-average ERA and WHIP, will be worth about 4.8 SGPs. You would expect the middle reliever to contribute only 0.8 SGPs during the balance of the year. The difference of 4.0 SGPs is worth about $172 (4.0 * $43 = $172), so this move is well worth the $20 in fees.

The critical factor to keep in mind as you apply this method is that the important assumptions other than the player projections — that is, the estimate of the dollar value of each SGP and the SGP formulas themselves — are based on average values for a large number of leagues. These average values may be appropriate for decisions in April and May, when it is too early to tell how the race in your league will shape up. As the season progresses, however, you should adjust these assumptions to reflect the realities of your league and your team's position in the race.

For example, if your team is clearly in contention for one of the top spots, the value of one SGP increases dramatically. In fact, if you could somehow be certain that your team would finish in the top half of our hypothetical league, then you could re-run the previous regression based on only the top six places and you would discover that one SGP would now be worth $117. At the other end of the spectrum, if you know your team will finish out of the money, then clearly the dollar value of one SGP will be zero, and you should refrain from making any further transactions.

Similarly, you may need to adjust the SGP formulas if the standings in a particular category in your league are unusually close or unusually spread out. If the RBI category is tightly bunched in your league in September and your team is battling for first, you may rightly decide that you want to spend $20 for Olmedo Saenz' four RBI after all.

Managing Your Roster with an In-Season Salary Cap

The in-season salary cap was one of the last major innovations to the official rules of Rotisserie, introduced in the late 1990s as an optional measure for leagues that carry over players from one season to the next. The in-season cap has proven effective in mitigating the long-standing problem of dumping, in which contending teams acquire high-priced stars from non-contending teams in exchange for low-priced future prospects.

Therefore, many carryover leagues have adopted in-season caps, presenting new challenges – and, for savvy owners, opportunities – in roster management. This essay discusses some of the implications of the in-season cap and offers suggestions on how to make the most of your capped roster.

Roto owners have always had to deal with a salary cap at one crucial point of the season – during the draft. Without an in-season cap, owners have the luxury of ignoring salaries once the draft ends (except perhaps when considering the implications of a transaction for future seasons).

With an in-season cap, some of the same thought processes that must be applied during the draft continue to be applicable throughout the season. That is, you must consider not just whether you want a certain player on your roster, but whether you want him on you roster at a given price. Salary dollars remain a limited resource throughout the season, and you must allocate them wisely.

A contending team typically increases its total salary during the season in three ways:

1. Trading
2. Purchasing free agents
3. Activating players from reserve lists

In all cases, of course, these transactions only increase total salary if the acquired or activated player has a higher salary than the player he is replacing, but this will tend to be the case for a contending owner who is trying to pack his roster with as much talent as possible.

Going into the draft, you know exactly how many dollars are available to be spent and what players are available. You can therefore estimate fairly precisely just how much value you should get for every dollar you spend.

When trying to estimate the value of salary dollars during the season, however, you cannot be nearly as precise. Although you know that each team will have an in-season cap of $40 above the draft budget (according to the official Rotisserie rules), you don't know how many teams will remain in contention and seek to use the entire amount of their salary cap. You would have an even tougher time estimating the additional player value that will become available to the contending teams through trades with out-of-contention teams, free agent purchases, and the emergence of players from team's reserve lists.

Although precise values will vary from league to league and season to season, in my observation, in-season salary cap dollars in a league with a "draft + $40" cap tend to be slightly more valuable than dollars at the draft. For example, if your AL Roto league has a $260 draft budget and a $300 in-season cap, contending teams will likely have the opportunity to accumulate a bit more than $300 worth of value on their roster as the season progresses, in terms of how players would be valued in your draft.

This assertion underscores the importance of good in-season salary management, because the only way to get more than $300 worth of draft value on your roster will be to manage your roster wisely. With that in mind, the following guidelines may help you maximize value under a salary cap:

Factor salaries into trading decisions and seek to trade for lower salaries. All else equal, a trade is clearly advantageous if you acquire less salary than you trade away. Swapping for a lower-priced player gives you more room under the salary cap to add other valuable players to your roster.

One less obvious implication of this concept is that a trade can be beneficial to you even if you give up a more valuable player for a less valuable player as long as the salary difference is great enough. Suppose in 2006 you traded a $34 Manny Ramirez for a $2 Reed Johnson. Over the course of the season, Ramirez was about $7 more valuable than Johnson, but the additional $32 of room under the cap you would have gained could have allowed you to add much more than $7 of additional value to your roster. This could have been a very good trade under the right circumstances (even ignoring the future-season benefit).

A rival owner may jump on the chance to acquire the more valuable player in this type of trade, particularly if he is not as aware of the impact of the cap. As a rule of thumb, try to gain at least twice the difference in salary as the difference in value lost between the players in the trade. And don't employ this tactic unless you already know how you are going to use the added salary capacity.

One final suggestion about trading for lower salaries: a particularly promising place to seek under-priced players is among those players in the last year of their contracts on out-of-contention teams. The owners of these teams, in looking to dump, are likely to be indifferent to the salary of the player they are trading. For the right package of prospects, you can gain a valuable player at a bargain salary.

Factor the salary cap into free agent bidding. You should always be trying to purchase free agents for as little as possible, but an in-season cap gives you one more reason to try to make the lowest winning bids you can. As your team's total salary approaches the cap during the course of the season, consider how different winning bids will affect your ability to make other transactions.

Will a certain bid take you so close to the cap that you won't be able to activate a key player when he comes off the DL? Will it put you so close to the cap that you will effectively be unable to bid for the next valuable free agent who becomes available? If so, you should feel confident that the player you are bidding on is worth that tradeoff or else you should lower your bid accordingly.

You can also improve your ability to cope with a salary cap by considering the following tactics on Draft Day:

Spend judiciously in the end game. When owners have too many dollars chasing too few players at the end of the draft, they typically spend whatever they have left to get the player they want. That makes sense in the absence of an in-season cap, but may not if your league has a cap. Suppose you and one other owner each have $5 left and each have just one catcher spot open. You may like one of the remaining available backup catchers a little better than the others, but don't spend $5 to get your preferred player. The catcher you prefer may be worth half a dollar more than the others, but you're better off settling for another reserve catcher for $1 and leaving yourself with an additional $4 of room under the salary cap to use throughout the season.

Pick up a "warm body" or two in the late reserve rounds. In leagues with deep reserve drafts, the late rounds are usually used to pick up minor league prospects. Instead, consider using one or two of your $2 reserve picks to stash away an extra hitter and/or a do-no-harm middle reliever whom you expect to be on a major league roster throughout the season. If you get into salary cap trouble during the season, the ability to activate one of these players may become quite valuable.

Playing for Next Year

If your Rotisserie league allows teams to carry players over from one season to the next, there comes a time when you have to shift your focus ahead to next year.

For the less fortunate, this day may arrive during the current season, when you face the harsh reality that your team is out of contention and you need to start rebuilding. Even contenders can savor their success for only a few days after the end of the regular season, then they too must think about the future. According to official Rotisserie rules, each team must cut down to a 23- or 25-man roster in October, after which winter waivers and unrestricted trading begin.

Determining whether to acquire a player for next year requires a different thought process than evaluating a trade for the current season. The player's salary becomes very important. Coming into 2007, Derrek Lee at $52 is virtually worthless (in a standard 12-team NL league). Freddy Sanchez at $3 is a steal.

When you hold a player on your roster over the winter, you are really holding an option to retain that player at his current salary. If the player is likely to go in the draft for less, that option is worthless. Why freeze Lee for $52 when you can almost certainly release him back into the pool and reacquire him in the draft for a lower price? A healthy Freddy Sanchez, though, might go for $15-20 or more, so the option to keep him for $3 is quite valuable. You can happily trade a $52 Lee for a $3 Sanchez if you are playing for next year.

Of course, we have no way of knowing in August or even in February just how much a player will cost in the upcoming draft. The best we can do is come up with a range of prices and probabilities as to where a player will likely fall in his range.

When I try to place a value on players for next season, I like to boil these factors down to a very simple formula:

Player's value for next year =
Upside draft price - Current salary

The player's "upside draft price" is an optimistic but reasonable assessment of what the player might go for in next year's draft. That is, what might the player cost if things go well for him between now and Draft Day?

Considering the upside potential is critical. Suppose two middle relievers have just completed statistically similar seasons and each carries a $2 salary. If one of the two has the potential to earn the closer's job in spring training while the other does not, then the first pitcher has a reasonable chance of going for a much higher price in your upcoming draft. Therefore, the option to keep the first pitcher for $2 is worth much more than the same option on the second pitcher.

Owners building for next year often focus on low-priced, younger players, but don't overlook the value in acquiring an established player at a higher salary. Alfonso Soriano may not seem like a bargain at $30, but his upside draft price for 2007 may be $40 or more. That makes the option on Soriano worth more than the option on a $2 rookie middle infielder who may be worth $6-8 in next year's draft.

If your Roto league is limited to the players in one of the major leagues, don't forget to factor in the possibility that a player may be in the other league next season, and therefore worthless to you. All other things being equal, a player signed to a long-term contract with a no-trade clause would be worth a little more than a player who will be a free agent, and hence may be headed to the other league.

When the time comes to play for next year, get the edge over your competitors by collecting the most valuable set of options.

Weighing Future Value against Current Value

As the current season marches on, Rotisserie owners considering trades are more likely to think about how any deal will affect their roster for the following season (assuming their league allows them to carry over players from year to year).

Of course, different owners will have different objectives in evaluating trades. Some Roto owners, with teams in tight pennant races, will care almost exclusively about improving their chance to win this year. Others, with teams hopelessly out of contention, will be concerned almost solely with strengthening their rosters for the next year. Still other owners will try to strike some sort of balance between the current and future impact of a deal.

In this essay, I will describe a method that allows you to quantify the tradeoffs involved in a deal that has implications beyond the current season. Regardless of your situation, you can use this method to determine the best way to achieve your objectives.

The method boils down to three steps:

1. Calculate the value you will gain or lose this season as a result of the trade.
2. Calculate the value you will gain or lose next season.
3. Combine those two values appropriately to calculate a total value for the trade.

This process is not quite as straightforward as it may appear because the calculation used to evaluate the current-season effect of a trade is rather different from the calculation used for a future season.

I discussed how to calculate the current-season impact of a trade in my essay "Revising Player Values During the Season." The basic idea is to estimate how many points you will gain or lose in your league's standings as a result of adding and removing players from your team. Once you complete this part of the analysis, you may conclude, for example, that a certain trade possibility will be likely to cost your team one point in the standings.

In analyzing the current-season value of a trade, the salaries of the players involved are irrelevant (unless your league has an in-season salary cap). But in evaluating the future-season value, the player salaries become critical.

The option to keep a player on your roster at the start of next season only has value if the player is likely to cost more in next year's draft than his current salary. If the player is likely to cost less than his current salary, there's no reason to freeze him on your roster next spring.

To simplify what is otherwise a more complicated analysis, I like to use this formula again to estimate a current value for the option to keep a player for next season:

Player's value for next year = Upside draft price - Current salary

The player's "upside draft price" is an optimistic but reasonable assessment of what the player might go for in next year's draft.

Let's consider a specific example from the 2006 NL season. Suppose another owner, who wants to add pitching, offers you Ryan Zimmerman for Roy Oswalt. You look at the expected performance of each player for the remainder of the season and consider how gaining Zimmerman and losing Oswalt will likely affect your team. You estimate that you'll lose about one point more by dealing Oswalt than you'll gain from picking up Zimmerman.

But Zimmerman, as a promising but unproven player, went for only $13 in your league's 2006 draft, while Oswalt, an established starter, cost $27. You estimate that Zimmerman has an upside draft price of about $23 for next year, while Oswalt's upside draft price is right in line with his 2006 price: $27. That means the value of Zimmerman's option for next year is $10 (23 -13 = 10), and the value of Oswalt's option is $0 (27 -27 = 0).

How, then, do you balance the results that this trade would likely cost you one point in the standings this year, but add $10 to the value of your roster for 2007?

First, we have to deal with the inconvenient fact that the units we have used to measure the current and future values are different. In the current season, we looked at standings points to gauge the trade, but for the future season, we considered salary dollars.

To equate these two measures, you can use a rule of thumb that one standings point is typically worth about $4 in the draft of a standard Roto league. In other words, the 10 extra dollars of value that you are likely to add to your roster next year if you freeze Zimmerman at $13 instead of Oswalt at $27 should be worth about 2.5 standings points for your team in 2007.

That brings you to the crucial step of your analysis: Would you rather lose one point this year to gain 2.5 next year — or not? To answer that question, you must return to your objectives.

If you have already decided either to go all out for this year or to throw in the towel, then the answer should be clear. If you would like to try to balance the two, I recommend putting a discount factor on the future value of the trade.

The discount factor reduces the future value for three reasons: 1) there's always a chance that your league won't continue next year, 2) there's always a chance that you won't continue in your league next year, and 3) a dollar today is always worth more than a dollar tomorrow.

If your league is established and stable, I suggest using a discount factor of 80%. In other words, count only 80% of the future-season value of the trade. If your league is relatively new or you think its future is in doubt, you may want to use a lower discount factor.

In the Zimmerman-for-Oswalt example, applying an 80% discount factor to the 2.5 standings points you expect to gain next year still yields 2.0 standings points, more than the one point you would be giving up this season. Of course, most owners will try to negotiate a better deal, but, if this is the best you can get, it still looks like a trade worth doing.

What to Root for

Albert Pujols had a big day today. The Cardinals first baseman went 3-for-5 with two HRs and five RBI.

If you have Pujols on your Rotisserie team, you have to be pleased with his performance. But just how pleased should you be? How much will his stats in today's game actually help your team at the end of the season? Would you rather have had Pujols' big game, or Carlos Zambrano's outing on the same day, in which he earned the win for the Cubs, pitching nine innings while allowing just six hits, two walks, and one earned run?

While it is almost always obvious whether a player has helped or hurt your team on a given day, you may not be aware of just how much he has helped or hurt. Being able to relate a player's performance in a single game, or even a single at-bat, to its impact on your league's final standings is beneficial for at least two reasons.

First, if you can accurately assess the ultimate impact of short-term player performance, you can make better roster management decisions. For example, if you are trying to decide whether to replace a catcher who has gone on the 15-day DL or whether to reserve a pitcher for his upcoming start in Colorado, it may help to understand just how much the anticipated incremental stats will help or hurt your team. If your league charges transactions fees, you may want to establish a threshold return on each dollar you spend to ensure that you are getting enough value for your money.

Second, knowing just how your players' individual at-bats and innings pitched are affecting your Roto team can enhance the fun, or at least the appreciation, of watching your players come up to bat and pitch every day during the season.

Fortunately, the SGP equations used to produce player dollar values can also be employed to calculate the marginal impact of each Rotisserie-relevant statistic that a player generates. For instance, we can apply the NL SGP equations from Chapter 3 to compute the standings gain points generated by each of Pujols' stats from today's game:

HR SGP
HR / 9.5 = 2 / 9.5 = 0.211

RBI SGP
RBI / 27.3 = 5 / 27.3 = 0.183

SB SGP
SB / 7.9 = 0 / 7.9 = 0

BA SGP
(((1611.366 + Hits) / (5946 + AB)) - 0.271) / 0.0015
= ((1611.366 / 5951) - 0.271) / 0.0015
= 0.000276 / 0.0015
= 0.184

In other words, since teams in standard NL Roto leagues are separated on average by 9.5 HRs in the HR category at year's end, Pujols' two HRs would be worth 0.211 points in the typical league standings. Likewise, his five RBI would gain his Roto team 0.183 points in that category. Since he did not steal a base, he had no effect on the SB category.

For computing the impact of Pujols' 3-for-5 performance on team BA, the concept is similar, but the formula is more complicated. Essentially, this formula says that Pujols' three hits in five at-bats would raise the BA of a typical team from .271000 to .271276. Since NL Roto teams are separated on average by .0015 in BA, Pujols' performance would add 0.184 points in the BA category.

In total then, Pujols' performance today was worth 0.211 + 0.183 + 0.184 = 0.578 SGPs.

(Those interested in the details of the equations will notice that the formula for BA presented here differs slightly from the one presented in Chapter 3. The formula presented in Chapter 3 measures the marginal effect of a player's entire season and is therefore based on a team's ABs before it acquires its last hitter. The formula here measures the marginal effect of only a few ABs and is hence based on a team's ABs including all hitters.)

We can perform a similar calculation to assess the impact of Zambrano's pitching performance:

W SGP
    W / 3.1 = 1 / 3.1 = 0.323

Sv SGP
    Sv / 6.2 = 0 / 6.2 = 0

ERA SGP
    (4.06 - ((601.33 + ER) / ((1333 + IP) / 9))) / 0.082
    = (4.06 - (602.33 / (1342 / 9))) / 0.082
    = (4.06 – 4.0395) / 0.082
    = 0.250

WHIP SGP
    (1.33 - ((1772.89 + H + BB) / (1333 + IP))) / 0.016
    = (1.33 - (1780.89 / 1342)) / 0.016
    = (1.33 - 1.32704) / 0.016
    = 0.185

Zambrano's performance produced 0.323 + 0.250 + 0.185 = 0.758 SGPs, so his day was somewhat more valuable to the typical Roto team than Pujols'.

For counting categories, like HRs and wins, the translation from statistics to SGPs is straightforward. Since 3.1 wins typically equate to one point in the standings, one win equates to 1/3.1 or 0.323 SGPs.

For rate categories, like BA and ERA, the relationship is less straightforward but not too difficult to unravel. For example, the average NL Roto team compiles 5946 ABs during a season, generating 1611.366 hits and a BA of .271.

Teams are typically separated in the BA category by .0015. Over 5946 ABs, this .0015 difference equates to 8.9 hits. So, a player who outperforms the average of .271 by 8.9 hits moves his team up one point in the standings; a player who outperforms by one hit moves his team up by 1/8.9 = 0.112 SGPs.

At the level of a single AB, if a hitter could get 0.271 hits, his AB would have no effect on his team. Of course, 0.271 hits is not a possible outcome; the only possible outcomes for a single AB, as far as BA is concerned, are zero hits or one hit.

If a hitter goes hitless in an AB, he has underperformed by 0.271 hits. At the end of the season, this shortfall of 0.271 hits can be expected to cost his team 0.271/8.9 = 0.030 SGPs. Conversely, if the hitter gets a hit, he has outperformed by 1 - 0.271 = 0.729 hits. That additional fractional hit can be expected to boost his team by 0.729/8.9 = 0.082 SGPs.

Following similar reasoning for ERA and WHIP, we can deduce that one additional earned run loses 0.082 SGPs, while one-third IP without an earned run gains 0.012 SGPs. One additional hit or walk costs 0.047 SGPs, while one-third IP without a hit or walk adds 0.021 SGPs.

These equations can be applied to any time period from a single play to a few weeks to evaluate ultimate standings impact. One interesting application is to answer that old Rotisserie quandary: When your pitcher is facing your hitter, what outcome should you root for? The answer is surprisingly complicated, and it depends on the specific situation and the eventual consequences of the plate appearance.

An out (without an RBI) is a nearly neutral event for your team. It costs you 0.030 SGPs in BA, but the one-third IP without an earned run or baserunner is worth a total of 0.033 SGPs.

On the other hand, a single (without a run scored) is initially a positive event, producing 0.082 SGPs in BA, while costing 0.047 SGPs in WHIP. The single, however, carries risk of further negative consequences for your pitcher in the form of earned runs or missing a win or save.

If the batter's single drives in an earned run for your pitcher, that makes matters worse. An earned run costs your team more than twice as much as an RBI benefits it (0.082 vs. 0.037 SGPs). Of course, if the run is unearned, the RBI becomes a net positive for your team, although you would still have to weigh that benefit against any risk that the run costs your pitcher a win or save.

A solo HR becomes a net positive for your team, even if the run is earned. The combined gain in HR, RBI, and BA is 0.224 SGPs, while the loss in ERA and WHIP is 0.129 points. Again, though, if the run jeopardizes a win or save for your pitcher, then you may still want to root against the HR.

Keep the following caveat in mind when applying these formulas to calculate SGPs: The formulas are based on the typical team in the typical league. They provide a useful measure, especially early in the season. But as your season unfolds, they may become less accurate for your team's situation. To take an extreme example, on the last day of the season, your team may be "locked in" to a certain number of points in some categories, while very small changes in stats may affect your standing in other categories. At that point, it clearly would not make sense to apply these formulas.

GLOSSARY

Alternative active player: When you are considering whether to exercise a current-season call option on Player X, the alternative active player is the guy whom Player X would be replacing on your active roster. When you are considering whether to exercise a put on Player X, the alternative active player is the guy who would replace Player X. In either case, the value of the alternative active player determines the exercise price of the option.

Auction inflation: A phenomenon observed in the auction in leagues that allow player carryover from one season to the next. Since owners will mostly choose to carry over good players at bargain salaries, there will be a higher ratio of marginal dollars to marginal SGPs available in the auction. As a result, dollar values for all players in the auction will be inflated compared to those in a league with no player carryover.

Baseline dollar: The $1 that you must spend to fill each slot on your roster. In the plural form, this term may refer to the minimum of $23 that each team must spend to fill its roster or to the $276 that all teams must spend in a standard 12-team league. (Contrast with "marginal dollar.")

Baseline SGPs: The standings gain points expected to be produced by the least valuable hitter and pitcher purchased in the auction. This value determines the minimum amount of player production that you will get if you spend only $1 — the baseline dollar — to buy a player. (Contrast with "marginal SGPs.")

Call option: In finance, a contract that gives one the right to purchase something at a pre-specified price. In Rotisserie baseball, an owner's right to move a player onto his active roster or to retain the player in a future season(s). (Contrast with "put option.")

Counting categories: Those categories in the Rotisserie standings that are calculated simply by adding up the number of times the statistic has been achieved by a team's players. In standard Roto, the counting categories are home runs, RBIs, stolen bases, wins, and saves. (Contrast with "rate categories.")

Current-season call option: An option to move a player onto your active roster during the current season. You have current-season call options on the players on your reserve list and possible current-season calls on the players in the free agent pool.

Current-season put option: An option to remove a player from your active roster during the current season. You have current-season put options on the players on your active roster.

Deflation factor: A number calculated and used during the auction to estimate how your dollar values have changed as a result of underbidding or overbidding for the players purchased so far. Ordinarily, other owners will pay too much (relative to your values) for players early in the auction, so there are fewer dollars left to buy the players remaining than your values would imply. Therefore, you must deflate your values by the deflation factor.

Discount factor: A number used to convert the value of something in the future, such as a call option to retain a player at the start of next season, to its appropriate present value.

Exercise (an option): To avail oneself of the right to buy or sell provided by an option.

Exercise price: The pre-specified price that you must pay if you exercise a call option, or the pre-specified price you receive if you exercise a put option.

Exercise price adjustment factor: A fudge factor in the shortcut approach to valuing future-season call options. We need this number because we cannot know in advance what a player's salary will be (or, therefore, the exercise price of his future-season calls).

Expected stats: A forecast of a player's stats comprising the average number that we expect the player to achieve in each category. Expected stats are the kind of player forecast used in Marginal SGP Pricing.

Expected value: The probability-weighted average of the possible values of a variable, equivalent to the mean or weighted average value of the variable.

Future upside (FUT UP): An optimistic estimate of the dollar value for a given player in next year's auction. The player should have a 20% chance of meeting or exceeding this dollar value; he will fail to do so 80% of the time. This number is used to value a player's future-season call option.

Future value: The value of an asset at that time in the future when you are able to possess or use the asset. In Rotisserie, if we determine what a future-season call option will be worth when we exercise it next spring, we are determining its future value. (Contrast with "present value.")

Future-season call option: An option to retain a player on your active or reserve roster at the start of next season (and possibly additional seasons beyond that). If you play in a league with player carryover, you will have a future-season call option on each player on your active and reserve rosters, unless the player is in the final year of his contract.

Future-season call baseline value: If your league allows player carryover, any player you purchase will come with a future-season call option. For most players, the value of this call is roughly equal to a low value that we refer to as the future-season call baseline value. In the shortcut approach to estimating option values, we do not give players credit for this baseline value, so we must subtract it from any option values we calculate.

Intrinsic value: The value that an option has if it were to be exercised immediately. For a Roto call option, the intrinsic value is equal to the value of the player being activated or retained minus the exercise price of the option. For a Roto put option, the intrinsic value is equal to the exercise price of the option minus the value of the player being removed from the active roster.

Marginal dollar: Any dollar that you choose to spend above the first dollar that you must spend on each player you purchase in the auction. In the plural form, this term may refer to the $237 that each team may spend, above the absolute minimum of $23, to fill its roster or to the $2844 that all teams may spend above the minimum of $276 in a standard 12-team league. (Contrast with "baseline dollar.")

Marginal SGPs: Any standings gain points a player is expected to produce above those expected to be produced by the least valuable player purchased in the auction. This value determines the amount of marginal dollars that you should be willing to spend to buy the player. (Contrast with "baseline SGPs.")

Marginal SGP Pricing: A method for calculating dollar values for players in a Rotisserie auction. The dollar value for each player depends primarily on the marginal SGPs he is expected to produce.

Option: In finance, a contract that gives one the right either to purchase or to sell something at a pre-specified price. A "call" option gives its holder the right to purchase something, and a "put" option gives its holder the right to sell something.

Option-adjusted dollar values: Dollar values for players in a Roto auction that reflect the value of the options that come with each player.

Option-Adjusted Marginal SGP Pricing: The Marginal SGP Pricing method enhanced to include the value of the options that come with each player.

Overpayment tally: A running total kept during the auction of how much owners have cumulatively overpaid for the players purchased so far. (If owners have underpaid, which would be quite unusual, the tally would be negative.) This number is used to calculate the deflation factor.

Position flexibility: A characteristic of a hitter who under Rotisserie rules qualifies at more than one position in the field. Also, a characteristic of a roster that has several such players. This characteristic can be valuable when making roster moves during the season.

Position scarcity: The condition that exists when the top 168 hitters available in the auction do not contain enough players at a certain position to fill all slots on each team's roster. Typically, there will be a shortage of catchers and perhaps middle infielders among the top 168 hitters. This condition affects dollar values for the auction, making players at the scarce positions more valuable.

Present value: The present value of an asset that you will not be able to use until sometime in the future. In Rotisserie, we must determine the present value of future-season call options, which we will not be able to exercise until next season or a subsequent season. (Contrast with "future value.")

Put option: In finance, a contract that gives one the right to sell something at a pre-specified price. In Rotisserie baseball, an owner's right to remove a player from his active roster. (Contrast with "call option.")

Rate categories: Those categories in the Rotisserie standings that are calculated on a per-opportunity basis. In standard Roto, the rate categories are batting average, earned run average, and WHIP. (Contrast with "counting categories.")

SGP denominator: A number that represents the expected additional production needed to finish one place higher in the standings for a given category. For instance, if you expect that a team will need about nine additional home runs to finish one place higher in the home run category in your league, then you should set your SGP denominator for home runs at nine.

Standings gain points (SGPs): A number used to represent the value of the contribution of any player to his team in Rotisserie baseball. SGPs are calculated by converting the player's production in each category into the number of points that production would gain for the average team in the standings.

Total SGPs: The total number of SGPs that a player is expected to produce, including both his baseline SGPs and his marginal SGPs.

Total SGP Pricing: A method for calculating dollar values for players in a Rotisserie auction that fails to distinguish between baseline SGPs and marginal SGPs. (Contrast with "Marginal SGP Pricing.")

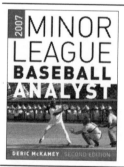
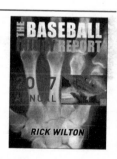